H. E. Robinson

The Eastern Question

In the Light of God's Promises to Israel

H. E. Robinson

The Eastern Question
In the Light of God's Promises to Israel

ISBN/EAN: 9783337126735

Printed in Europe, USA, Canada, Australia, Japan

Cover: Foto ©Lupo / pixelio.de

More available books at **www.hansebooks.com**

Preface.

THIS book has an object; and this object we invite the reader to consider for a moment before entering upon a perusal of the work. The object is to throw the search-light of prophecy upon one of the greatest and most important questions now agitating the world. That question is the Eastern Question. You are already interested in that question, as every one is, who has an intelligent acquaintance with the great political movements of the present day. But your interest will be greatly increased by looking at it in the light of prophecy; because prophecy throws upon it an illumination which goes far beyond any natural foresight and human deductions. It shows the startling results of the movements involved in this controversy. The human view sees only a change in the map of Europe, and the disappearance of Turkey as a political factor in the national agitations of this world; the prophetic view sees the disappearance, not of Turkey alone, but of all the nations of the earth, and the establishment of God's everlasting kingdom, as the true solution, and the immediate result of the settlement of this great question. How this is to be brought about, the author of this work clearly shows. The subject being thus presented from the true point of view, every one will be enabled to see his own personal concern in the matter, in reference to his spiritual and eternal interests.

But more than this, the presentation of this truth in this manner, exposes an error, now widely spread through Christendom, which is misleading thousands in their conceptions of the future. To be enlightened in regard to the grand scheme of God's purposes among men, and to be in harmony with his work, is the most exalted position one can occupy in this world; and believing that this little work will be a help to many in reaching that position, we are happy to send it forth upon its mission of light and love. PUBLISHERS.

Contents.

	PAGES
INTRODUCTION, ...	9–14

Subject defined — Nations perplexed — Divine information — God's care for Israel — Questions concerning the Hebrew nation.

CHAPTER ONE.

THE ISRAEL OF GOD, ... 15–25

Origin of name "Israel" — Who are Jews? — Abraham's "seed" identified — Literal and spiritual Israel — General remarks.

CHAPTER TWO.

THE HEBREW NATION, ... 26–43

Difference between the true Israel and the national Israel — History of the Hebrews — Division of the kingdom — Captivity of Israel and Judah — "Ten lost tribes" — The restoration — Nation reunited — Final dispersion — Theory concerning the return of the Jews — God's Promises to Israel — Conversion of the Jews — An Impressive Lesson — Character of true Israel.

CHAPTER THREE.

THE GENTILE NATIONS, ... 44–63

Equality of all men before God — His unchangeable plan in the gospel — Call of Abraham — Divine purpose with reference to the Hebrew nation — Their rebellious disposition — Rejection of the nation — Individual salvation — Gentiles called — Equal terms to Jews and Gentiles; both must alike become true Israel by faith — Christians and Israelites compared — National boasting prohibited — Manner of saving all Israel — Blindness of Jews — Gentile fulness.

[5]

CHAPTER FOUR.

THE HEATHEN NATIONS, . . . 64–78

God's dealing with the heathen — Responsibility measured by light imparted — Gospel revealed in nature — Design of the Sabbath — Who are heathen?

CHAPTER FIVE.

UNIVERSAL RESTORATION, . . . 79–89

Truth and error contrasted — Israel compared with Sodom, Samaria, and Satan — Logical extent of restoration theories — Sin against the Holy Ghost — No forgiveness in a future age — Paul's sorrow for his kinsmen.

CHAPTER SIX.

"ANOTHER GOSPEL," . . . 90–101

Early advocates of Hebrew pre-eminence — Paul's curse on such teaching — Modern parallel — Dispensational salvation — God's elect — Theories concerning the bride — True Israel, the church, the elect people, and Christians — Unity of the faith — One body of believers in all ages — Mutilating scriptures — Fruits of error.

CHAPTER SEVEN.

THE PROMISED LAND, . . . 102–113

Location of Israel's inheritance — Three worlds — Destruction of the old world — God's purpose in creation — Covenant with Noah — The rainbow token — The present evil world — The world to come — New earth promised to Abraham — A heavenly country — The New Jerusalem — Paradise restored.

CHAPTER EIGHT.

THE SANCTUARY, ... 114–138

Important historical connections — A subject of prophecy — Daniel 8 : 14 — Theory concerning the sanctuary and its cleansing — What is the sanctuary? — Original command — Building erected by Moses — Its purpose defined — A pattern of things in heaven — Christ's work as priest — Objections considered — Cleansing the typical sanctuary — Application of symbols to the real service of Christ — Last ministration of grace to sinners — 2300 days — Explained by seventy weeks — A day for a year — Period ended in 1844 — Intermediate dates and events — Perpetual desolation which befell national Israel — Rome the desolater — Strange theory concerning the seventieth week.

CHAPTER NINE.

THE KINGDOM OF CHRIST, . . . 139–154

Relation to the Eastern Question — Popular methods advocated — Ballot-box religion — Testimony of Christ — This world not the kingdom — A monstrous fable — A magnificent price offered for one vote — The throne of David — Difference between Melchisedec and David — Close of probation to all the race — Finishing the mystery of God — The Judgment.

CHAPTER TEN.

THE DOOM OF TURKEY, . . . 155–170

Turkey the center of the Eastern Question — All nations involved — Turkey in prophecy — Called the "king of the north" in Daniel 11 — Direction of Turkey's chief troubles — His reckless course foretold — Expulsion from Europe predicted — Final stand at Jerusalem — Comes to his "end" — Michael — Christ takes his kingdom — A time of trouble to all the world — True Israel delivered — Armageddon.

CHAPTER ELEVEN.

TURKEY AND RUSSIA, . . . 171–183

Rise of Othman — Character of his government — Five months' "torment" — Subsequent command to "slay" — Capture of Constantinople, 1453 — Period of Turkey's independent rule — Fall of the Ottoman Empire, 1840 — Quotation from *Public Ledger* — Extracts from Ridpath's History — Last will of Peter the Great — The Crimean war — Turko-Russian war of 1877 — England's Turkish policy — Statement of Lord Salisbury.

CONTENTS.

CHAPTER TWELVE.

THE MODERN CRUSADE, . . . 184-198
False Standard of Christianity — Satan's Part in the Eastern Question — Popular expectations a matter of prophecy — What "many people" say — What the Lord says.

CHAPTER THIRTEEN.

THE DAY OF THE LORD, . . . 199-214
Indications of its proximity — Manner of its approach — A period of darkness — Decree which closes the gospel message — The seven last plagues — Righteous Israel delivered — The eagles and the carcass — Coming of Christ.

CHAPTER FOURTEEN.

THE FOUR WINDS, ... 215-226
Winds a symbol of war — Held so that Israel may be sealed — Compared with the history of the Eastern Question — The final whirlwind — Elijah the prophet — The hour of judgment message — Fall of Babylon — The last warning.

CHAPTER FIFTEEN.

THE SECOND EXODUS, . . . 227-246
Object teaching — Dispersion of true Israel — Persecution their lot — Dragon makes war on the remnant — Christian Sabbath keepers — Promises of Israel's gathering — Time and manner of their return — The righteous dead resurrected — Valley of dry bones — A physical change.

CHAPTER SIXTEEN.

THE MILLENNIUM, ... 247-263
Description in Revelation 20 — Two resurrections — Inheritance in heaven — Saints judge the world — Earth desolate — Satan bound — Satan loosed — The second death.

CHAPTER SEVENTEEN.

THE ROYAL FAMILY, . . . 264-276
Christ and the church — The bride — An allegory — Joy of redeemed Israel — Unmeasured grace of God.

THE EASTERN QUESTION.

INTRODUCTION.

THE Eastern Question is a well-known, world-wide expression, representing one of the most important and interesting issues now before mankind. Religion and politics, the church and the state, are all involved in the complications grouped under this comprehensive title. The happiness, the existence even, of individuals, nations, and the world, is linked together, and trembling in the balance which a breath may move. In thought and speech, public and private; in pulpit, platform, and press; in every nation and continent of the earth, the Eastern Question is recognized as the foremost subject now before the world. The following pages will show that it deserves and rightfully demands such attention.

The Eastern Question has come to stay. Willingly or unwillingly, its claims must be met and an answer given. No conjuring will banish the form rising in the East, which appears to the nations as an alarming specter, but to the church as a sign of the fulfilment of her fondest hopes. For half a century it has kept millions of armed men in constant training for deadly combat, and still they dare not sleep. The cloud first seen as the hand of a man in extent has now spread its dark pall over the heavens. Everybody speaks of it with feelings of dread.

What is the Eastern Question? Like other apparitions, this is hard to define. It means so much, and yet so little. The thing itself is only a shadow, but on the minds of men it sits like an incubus of crushing weight. No one can clearly describe the object as it appears to his vision. Each nation views it in a different light from all others. In the language of a well-known author who wrote about thirty years ago, we may say, "To Russia it may mean one thing, to France another, and to Austria still another; but sifted of every side issue, it may be reduced to this,— THE DRIVING OF THE TURK INTO ASIA, and a scramble for his territory." This was the condition then, and it has not changed in general features since, except to become more comprehensive, until now it virtually means *driving the Turk off the earth, and a rush for his territory in Asia as well as in Europe.*

The situation at present may be summed up in the following words: The empire of Turkey occupies one of the most fertile and historic regions of the world in two continents, and controls the highway of trade between the Black Sea and the Mediterranean, thus depriving Russia on the north of harbors for commerce and ports for fleets of war.

In other words, Turkey is not only a rich prize in herself to her greedy neighbor, but she also stands in the way of his ambitions concerning other rival powers. These with other causes have made Russia the implacable foe of Turkey, and it is no secret that the great northern empire is determined to secure a portion at least of the possessions belonging to his southern neighbor. A conflict between these two opposing powers alone would be of short duration. Turkey is weak and despotic, detested at home and abroad. Russia is strong and despotic, feared at home and abroad. The so-called "Sick Man" could not withstand the hug of the "Bear" if they were to meet for a final encounter.

In this unequal struggle, the great powers of Central and Western Europe have interposed to keep the sultan on the throne of Turkey, and to restrain the advance of Russia. It is not an unselfish policy; each is jealous of the others, and fearful that if a powerful government should reign in Constantinople, the balance of power would be broken, and the equilibrium of Europe destroyed. No danger from this source is feared while Turkey remains in possession. Therefore, over the affairs of Turkey and the mutual distrust of other nations, the Eastern Question has developed until all Europe is involved. All have discovered that they must ultimately "fight for peace," and preparations for the contest have gone on without intermission, till the earth trembles beneath the hosts marshaling for the fray.

Meanwhile the Turk is making no end of trouble for his guardians. By heredity, education, and religion he is a scourge to the race. His sponsors have done their best to keep him in check, so that the peace of Europe may not be interrupted, but massacre after massacre in his dominions has frozen the blood and sealed the lips of his former friends. All the civilized world instinctively feels that his national doom is near, and the people have made numerous petitions to their respective governments asking that further support shall be withdrawn and the culprit left to his fate.

But just here rises the dread of future results, if once the hold is loosed. Who can tell what will follow? The issue is dark. If the Turk is left to his fate, what will be the effect? Will peace ensue, and the several rival powers disband their troops? or will the long-pent-up volcano of war burst out if the pressure is at all relaxed? Well may the statesmen pause, even though goaded to action by an impatient populace. The problem is full of mystery and uncertainty. Is the long-looked-for time of peace about to dawn, or are new horrors about to arise from this Eastern Question? O, if there were some divine oracle, some flashing Urim and Thummim, some prophet of the Lord, where we might inquire concerning all these wonders!

And here is the only ray of hope. If God has spoken to the troubled earth in reference to these matters, all is well for those who hear his voice. Is the cloud, so dark toward Egypt, light toward the promised land? Has the sure word of prophecy given us history in advance to guide our feet along the dim pathway? On the sacred pages are recorded the story of the nations of old time; do they also speak to men of present affairs? With unerring accuracy they pointed out the dangers then, unheeded by the rushing crowd; let them but speak once more, and we will listen. Yes; God has spoken of these very days. These current events are recorded for our benefit. He still holds out the scepter of love, as low we kneel before the throne of grace. His word shall be our guide, his will our law, his truth our shield and buckler.

Where shall we begin to trace the footsteps of Jehovah among the Babel paths of men? Where, indeed, except with that chosen people, for whose sake "the Most High divided to the nations their inheritance; when he separated the sons of Adam, he set the bounds of the people according to the number of the children of Israel." Amid all the changing empires and dynasties of time, the God of Abraham, Isaac, and Jacob is working out his eternal purpose for "Israel." Their welfare is bound up in this Eastern Question, and for their sakes the light is given along the ages to come. Give an attentive ear to their story as told in the following pages; for with their destiny is involved the world's fate.

The Hebrew nation once inhabited Palestine, with Jerusalem for their capital city. To-day they are scattered in all lands, and the disciples of a false religion now occupy the places of sacred memory. Is the Turk to be driven out? Are the scattered Hebrews to be gathered back to Judea, and re-established in their ancient inheritance? Is Christ to reign on David's throne at Jerusalem? Will a millennium of peace on earth be realized? When, where, and how will the "sanctuary be cleansed"? What will be the condition of Gentile nations when the promises to Israel are fulfilled? etc., etc. All these and many more inquiries are parts of the world's great problem called the Eastern Question, and all are answered in the Holy Scriptures. The questions and answers are coupled together in this little volume. No one can truly understand the course of events who does not trace God's dealings with Israel; hence much of our space will be devoted to this theme.

CHAPTER ONE.

THE ISRAEL OF GOD.

NO one will deny that there are many promises to Israel which pertain to the future, and that they will all be exactly fulfilled in due time. But in their fulfilment the whole earth and all the people upon it are involved, and so through them the Eastern Question and every other question is open for study.

In the discussion of any subject it is necessary that the terms employed should be clearly understood. Otherwise misunderstanding will arise, and discord will ensue. Our first duty, therefore, is to ascertain who are meant in the Scriptures by the words "Israel," "Jew," "Abraham's seed," and similar expressions. Modern use restricts these titles to one particular nation — the Hebrew people. Does the Bible universally apply them in that way? What meaning is attached to them by the Lord? It will at once be seen that this is a vital point. God's definition and application must be followed, if we would understand his promises. We are not at liberty to attach an arbitrary interpretation to these names. Many conclude without investigation that the commonly received meaning of these words is the same as the Bible gives to them. But this should by no means be taken for granted. If a wrong base is laid at the start, the whole structure will suffer, notwithstanding the infinite labor bestowed on the dome. Therefore before we can understand the promises to Israel, we must first ascertain who are Israel in the mind of God. On this point the following testimony is ample : —

The name "Israel" is defined as "a prince of God." It is first used in the Bible in Gen. 32 : 28. From its use on this occasion we may learn its meaning, by noticing the following circumstances: Jacob, as the name indicates, was a tricky, dishonest man, who had supplanted his brother, Esau, deceived his father, Isaac, and outwitted his uncle, Laban. While thus guilty, he set out to return to his boyhood home after an absence of twenty years. On the journey, he was attacked one dark and lonely night by what appeared to be a robber bent on murder. Jacob wrestled for his life until the morning began to dawn. Then by a mysterious touch from his unknown antagonist, Jacob's thigh was put out of joint, and he could struggle no more. But the same moment that Jacob saw his helplessness, he also saw the Lord as his adversary — the same One he had seen in his dream at Bethel when he fled an exile from his father's house. Hope immediately took the place of fear, and to the Lord's apparent intention to depart, Jacob, now humbled and penitent, exclaimed, "I will not let thee go, except thou bless me." His confession of sin is shown more fully in the words of Hosea 12 : 3-5 : "He took his brother by the heel in the womb, and by his strength he had power with God. Yea, he had power over the angel, and prevailed; he wept, and made supplication unto him; he found him in Bethel, and there he spake with us; even the Lord God of Hosts; the Lord is his memorial." Jacob's faith gave him victory with the Lord. He was then a converted man, a new creature in Christ Jesus. Then the Lord bestowed a new name on the new man: "And he said unto him, What is thy name? And he said, Jacob. And he said, Thy name shall be called no more Jacob, but Israel; for as a prince hast thou power with God and with men, and hast prevailed."

From this we learn that Jacob was not "Israel" by being born of Hebrew parents. Only by the pardon of his sin could he receive the title of "a prince of God," and the name "Israel" was conferred upon him by the Lord himself. Applying these principles in a general way, the conclusion follows that no person is an Israelite in the true and primary sense of the word by being born of Hebrew ancestors; that this distinction relates to a righteous character, received by faith; and that God only can bestow it on those who are "born from above." Israel is a title which cannot be transmitted from an earthly father to his son; but it must come from the Heavenly Father, and is given to those alone who become children of God. Here is a difference often overlooked in common speech; people are called Israelites by men, simply because they are Hebrews; but in the sight of God no man is an Israelite by human descent. Natural birth, physical form, and national language have nothing to do with the matter. The features of a true Israelite are a contrite, humble heart, which only God can see. This agrees with the words of Christ concerning Nathanael, "Behold an Israelite indeed, in whom is no guile;"[1] also with Paul's language: "For in Christ Jesus neither circumcision availeth anything, nor uncircumcision, *but a new creature*. And as many as walk according to this rule, peace be on them and mercy, and upon the Israel of God."[2] Here, then, is the "rule" given by the Holy Spirit and applied by the apostle: A person must be a "*new creature*," in order to be classed among the "Israel of God." That same "rule" holds good to-day, and men have no right to use any other in measuring God's chosen people.

This is not saying that in the Bible the word "Israel" always means converted men. On the contrary, the term often designates a certain race of people without reference to character. But the former is the original and correct application, while the other is a secondary use of the word. In all cases where it is consistent with the context and circumstances recorded, the primary definition

[1] John 1: 47.   [2] Gal. 6: 15, 16.

should be understood. An example of both meanings is found in the use of the word "Christian." Strictly speaking, a person is a Christian only when converted to Christ; but the word is often used now to designate a whole nation, even though a large majority make no profession of being Christ's followers. No one will claim that all are Christians who belong to so-called "Christian nations." In like manner the word "Israel" is sometimes employed to describe a nation when perhaps but a very few are Israelites in the true sense. Hence Paul could declare, "*For they are not all Israel which are of Israel.*"

By ignoring the fact that the promises of future blessings to Israel refer to those only who are Christ's indeed, many writers and teachers have framed erroneous theories concerning the Hebrew nation, and so of course are entirely wrong in their conclusions about the Eastern Question. Therefore we emphasize the statement that the reader must clearly discern this distinction, and apply it properly, in order to avoid untold confusion. In harmony with the foregoing, notice how the word "Jew" has a double use.

WHO ARE JEWS?

The Lord's description of a "Jew" is similar to that of an Israelite: "For he is not a Jew, which is one outwardly; neither is that circumcision, which is outward in the flesh; but he is a Jew, which is one inwardly; and circumcision is that of the heart, in the spirit, and not in the letter; whose praise is not of men, but of God."[1] No one can misunderstand these statements. The name "Jew," like "Israel," is a sacred title which God alone can give. When the Lord applies it, the man has "praise of God;" when mere men give that name to a person or people, it is simply "praise of men," and amounts to nothing, except to show that those who use it and those who receive it in this manner, do not really know whom the Lord calls a Jew. Let the Hebrew of to-day beware of those who would flatter him as a special subject of God's favor because of his natural descent; and let those who thus apply the term to unconverted men, as proof that special blessings are promised to them in this or a future age, be careful lest the blood of deceived souls shall be found upon them. Let God's idea of a Jew be taught, and more will desire the praise of that name from divine lips. It is astonishing how carelessly these words are now applied to all classes of men, until their real significance is nearly lost. But God has not changed, and he knows those who are really his, and also those "which say they are Jews, and are not, but do lie."

ABRAHAM'S SEED.

The same general principles which pertain to the true Israelite, or Jew, are equally applicable to

[1] Rom. 2:28, 29.

those whom the Lord recognizes as "Abraham's seed." The name "Abraham" did not come by natural descent from any man. "Abram" was the appellation bestowed by the human parents to designate their son born of the flesh. No honor in God's sight comes through that source. Christ says, "The flesh profiteth nothing;" and Paul writes, "So then they that are in the flesh cannot please God;" and he applies this truth to the particular case of Abraham in the words, "What shall we say then that Abraham our father, as pertaining to the flesh, hath found?" and then proceeds to answer the question by stating that all he received came to him by believing God. "Without faith it is impossible to please God." Then so far as men are concerned, faith is the only avenue to God's favor. In this way Abram became the friend of God, and his name was changed to Abraham, "the father of all them that believe." Thus, over and over again the important lesson is taught that no permanent blessing can come to any person without the exercise of faith on his part.

Likewise the "seed" of Abraham derive nothing from the fleshly birth. This is made very plain by noticing the difference between the two sons, Ishmael and Isaac. The former was born "after the flesh," the latter "after the Spirit." In reference to them the Lord said: "Cast out the bondwoman and her son; for the son of the bondwoman shall not be heir with the son of the freewoman. So then, brethren, we are not children of the bondwoman, but of the free."[1] It is therefore certain that the natural descendants from Abraham are all Ishmaelites in God's sight, and only those who have been begotten by the direct power of God are counted for the seed through Isaac. Notice this same conclusion in exact Scripture: "Neither, because they are the seed of Abraham, are they all children; but in Isaac shall thy seed be called. That is, they which are the children of the flesh, these are not the children of God; but the children of the promise are counted for the seed."[2]

LITERAL AND SPIRITUAL.

An objection to the foregoing conclusions is sometimes made by saying that the promises yet to be fulfilled can apply only to a "*literal* Israel," whereas in these texts, a "*spiritual* Israel" is represented. The difficulty in this case all arises from a wrong idea of the words "spiritual" and "literal." The former is supposed to denote intangible, immaterial beings, of spiritual essence, inhabiting an invisible world; while the latter refers to real persons of flesh and blood, capable of happiness on this material planet. Therefore, as many promises do relate to material things, like the "land," the "city," etc., the assertion is made that they cannot be fulfilled to the spiritual Israel, but that some literal nation or people must be intended. In subsequent portions of this book it

---

[1] Gal. 4:22-31.   [2] Rom. 9:7, 8.

will be shown how all these conditions are in exact harmony with the plain facts already learned concerning true Israel. In this connection, therefore, we merely remark that *spiritual* things are *literal*, but they are not *carnal*. Spiritual beings are not ghosts, nor disembodied souls of men. They are real persons. Heaven is just as literal as earth; angels are as literal as men. The "things which are seen are temporal; but the things which are not seen are eternal." Then it is a fact that eternal things are actually more real than the temporal. The true Israelite is a literal human being. In the present life he has flesh and blood like other men. For the life to come he looks to the "Saviour, the Lord Jesus Christ, who shall change our vile body, that it may be fashioned like unto his glorious body."[1] Christ, after his resurrection, was a real, literal being, with hands, feet, sides, etc.; able to converse, eat food, and do any act of which mortal persons are capable. True Israel, the redeemed saints out of all nations, will be made like him; therefore they will be able to "dwell in the land," eat the food it produces, and enjoy all its blessings. Individuals do not become spiritual Israel by dying and laying aside the physical body; but those who have died must live again before they can inherit the earth.

Christ confounded the Sadducees, and proved the resurrection of the dead, by citing the fact that God is not the God of the dead but of the living;

---
[1] Phil. 3:21.

and as he is the God of Abraham, Isaac, and Jacob, who were then and are now dead, they must be raised to life. Therefore true Israel will always be a real, tangible, literal people, though finally made immortal. Now, they are saved Israel, by the Spirit dwelling in corruptible flesh; then, they will be redeemed Israel, by the same Spirit inhabiting incorruptible flesh. One condition is just as literal as the other, and both are *spiritual*. *Grasp the fact so plainly stated, that only those who are truly Christ's are Israelites indeed; hold it fast in all this discussion, and perfect harmony with each and all the accompanying conditions will be the glorious result.*

GENERAL REMARKS.

Much more concerning Israel is yet to be presented in following chapters, confirming and enlarging the conclusions now reached; but before we turn from this division, let us review the statements already made. We are face to face with the Eastern Question. This subject is intimately related to the people of Israel, as will more fully appear in subsequent pages. Therefore we ask, Who are meant by Israel?—From plain words of inspiration we learn that the term "Israel" is not confined to any nation, either Hebrew or Gentile; in fact, these worldly associations are a hindrance instead of being a help. On the contrary, we find that Israel is the title of those who are "in the world, but not of the world." They are the truly converted followers of Christ. Birth, wealth, education, or any other endowment of men, does not constitute a mark of God's people. All the promises of the gospel are made to the Israel of God, and no promise for the future is made to a Gentile. These are not statements made to support a human theory of national pride, but they are facts of great weight. We do not deny that there is a literal Israel in the world; but God alone can tell who they are, for he looks at the heart. We do not deny the promises yet unfulfilled to the chosen people; "for all the promises of God in him are yea, and in him amen, unto the glory of God by us." We have one point settled, and this is a key which will unlock every door we shall meet. Without it, men wander in the maze of speculation. True Israel does not mean the "Hebrew nation," the "ten lost tribes," the "Anglo-Saxon race," nor any other division of natural men. It does mean a literal people, "born again," composed of some individuals out of every nation and tongue under heaven. Here is solid rock on which to build for the future. All theories in opposition to these Scriptural facts rest on a foundation of sand, or are merely floating castles in the air.

Chapter Two.

THE HEBREW NATION.

OUR readers will bear in mind that the name "Israel" is used in two ways in the Scriptures. One designates God's true people out of every nation; the other denotes all or part of the Hebrew nation alone, without respect to moral character. The first is the original and primary meaning; the second is a restricted and temporary term. This prominent distinction is not always mentioned when the word is used; but the careful student will have little difficulty in making a right application in each particular instance, if both definitions are kept in mind, and the one used which is consistent with the context and other passages of the Bible. Some modern writers forget or ignore these obvious facts, and foolishly endeavor to apply all such statements to one and the same class, thus leading to extravagant and fanciful interpretations and monstrous conclusions. Texts which, rightly understood, point out the superlative glory of the redeemed saints in the world to come, are thus made to figure grotesquely in picturing the lofty pre-eminence of some powerful governments in this present evil world. Blessings promised to true

Israel and curses pronounced on apostate Israel are mingled, and quoted at random to fit any theory extant. Much Scripture is employed, but the application is entirely wrong. These expositors pass over the real Israel as described in the Lord's own word, and labor to show that some nation or race of natural men is the object of every prediction. Nothing but error and confusion can possibly come from such attempts. We therefore hope that the candid reader will clearly comprehend this vital matter, and use this knowledge in our further study. In the previous chapter the Israel of God was the special theme; in this one the national Israel, or the Hebrew tribes, will be considered. It will be assumed that the reader is somewhat familiar with the political history of this people, and that therefore minute details are unnecessary.

For many centuries the Hebrews were under the Lord's direct instruction and discipline. At first the whole nation was distinguished by the general name of Israel, composed of twelve tribes. In the course of time ten tribes revolted, and formed a separate government, retaining the name "Israel," while the remaining portion was usually called "Judah." The subsequent career of both factions was marked by deep apostasy and final captivity. A portion of the ten tribes of Israel were first removed into Assyria and placed in certain cities of Media, while people from the various Assyrian provinces were taken to Samaria and put in the place of the Hebrew captives. About one hundred years later the kingdom of Babylon rose to the zenith of power under Nebuchadnezzar, and all the old Assyrian Empire came under his sway. Thus the people of Israel came under the rule of Babylon. About the same time the kingdom of Judah also was conquered by Nebuchadnezzar, and some of its inhabitants were carried captives to Babylon. The entire Hebrew nation, both Israel and Judah, was thus represented in the captivity in Babylon, as well as by the portion of each that was left in their respective countries of Samaria and Judea. Many of the people in captivity became gradually assimilated with their conquerors in the various provinces, so that their tribal relations were obliterated, and their genealogy lost.

LOST ISRAEL.

In no true sense did the whole ten tribes become "lost." There is not sufficient evidence to prove that these tribes remained in a consolidated form, and finally migrated in a body to other lands, where they have recently been "discovered" and "identified" in the Anglo-Saxon race. Every natural circumstance in the case forbids such a supposition. Without express and positive testimony to the contrary, the only rational view is that they became absorbed to some extent in the nations where they lived. The strenuous efforts made in some quarters to trace them to the English-speaking nations, or to other European powers, is an example of painful and reckless prophetic and historic exposition. Glowing descriptions of the true Israel of God, gathered at last from a world of sin into a new earth redeemed from the curse, have been tortured into a theory to uphold national pride in governments and conditions existing at the present time. If selfish, ambitious nations were persuaded that they were the special favorites of heaven to conquer and possess the land of Palestine, it would follow that the driving out of the Turk and the settlement of the Eastern Question would be necessary steps to fulfil the predictions, and plenty of excuses for a "righteous war" would soon be invented. This would be exactly parallel with the reported proceedings of an ecclesiastical body which gravely —

Resolved, That the Lord has given this earth to the saints; and further,—

Resolved, That we are the saints.

Fortunately for the world, political leaders and civil rulers are generally men of good sense, who are not easily stampeded into a rush to the Holy Land by the religious enthusiasts who have theories of such brilliant conquests. While these extreme views are not advocated extensively at the present time by the conservative religious bodies, there is quite a general idea that the future developments in gospel work will center at Jerusalem, and no doubt this will have some influence on the final settlement of the Eastern Question in that region. Again we assert that a correct regard for the true Israel will prevent the absurd claims of those who teach the Anglo-Israel doctrine that the ten tribes were once lost, but are now found. This will more fully appear as we proceed now to speak of —

THE RESTORATION.

After seventy years' captivity in Babylon, as before noted, we come to the several decrees made for Israel's restoration to their own land. The first of these was made by Cyrus in the year 536 B. C., and recorded in the first chapter of the book of Ezra. This was confirmed by a later Persian king, Darius Hystaspes by name, and greatly extended by a third Persian ruler called Artaxerxes Longimanus. The Persian Empire at that time embraced all that had formerly belonged to Babylon, besides other territory, as stated in Esther 1:1, "An hundred and seven and twenty provinces," "from India even unto Ethiopia." Every place where Israel and Judah had gone was thus included in the royal proclamation. This is shown by the following quotation from the decree of Cyrus: —

Thus saith Cyrus king of Persia, The Lord God of heaven hath given me all the kingdoms of the earth; and he hath charged me to build him an house at Jerusalem, which is in Judah. Who is there among you of all his people? his God be with him, and let him go up to Jerusalem, which is in Judah, and build the house of the Lord God of Israel (he is the God) which is in Jerusalem.[1]

[1] Ezra 1:2, 3.

Under this permission, about 50,000 persons returned to Jerusalem. We are not directly told that the ten tribes of Israel returned to Palestine at this time; but they were certainly included in the king's decree, and it was entirely their own fault if they did not return with the others. Many of them, no doubt, preferred to stay in the places where they had so long lived in honorable captivity. But the conclusion must not be drawn that *none* from Israel as distinguished from Judah, returned to their own land at this or later migrations; for there is plain Scripture evidence to the contrary, besides the natural tendencies which would operate in the same direction. In other words, it is certain that Israel, as well as Judah, was represented in the movement, and thus the twelve tribes, or all the Hebrew nation, were included in the restoration. Ten tribes were not "lost" at that time, while only two returned, but some out of all the tribes went to Palestine, as the following quotation shows : —

And the *children of Israel*, the priests, and the Levites, and the rest of the children of the captivity, kept the dedication of this house of God with joy, and offered . . . *for all Israel, twelve he goats, according to the number of the tribes of Israel.* . . . And the children of Israel, which were come again out of captivity, . . . kept the feast of unleavened bread seven days with joy; for the Lord had made them joyful, and turned the heart of the king of Assyria unto them, to strengthen their hands in the work of the house of God, the God of Israel.[1]

[1] Ezra 6 : 16-22

Let particular notice be given to the facts as stated in these verses. "The children of Israel, which were come again out of captivity," are directly mentioned, and it is asserted that the Lord turned the heart of the king of Assyria to favor them in this matter. Also that "all Israel" were represented in the offering of the twelve goats according to the number of the tribes of Israel. Similarly in Ezra 8 : 35 it is stated that "twelve bullocks for all Israel" were offered. Also in the decree of Artaxerxes special mention is made of the "people of Israel" in the permission to return, and Ezra expressly states that he "gathered together out of Israel chief men to go up with" him.[1] What excuse can be made for those who in the face of these words of God declare that the ten tribes of Israel were lost in Assyria, so that only the two tribes of Judah and Benjamin returned to Jerusalem? Only blind adherence to a cherished theory will lead men thus to disregard palpable facts. Let no one be deceived by any "lost Israel" story.

THE HEBREW NATION REUNITED.

Furthermore, the name "Israel" is frequently applied to the Hebrew people who inhabited Judea and Jerusalem after the return from captivity even down to their final dispersion by the armies of Rome. On the day of Pentecost Peter addressed his words to the "men of Israel" who had crucified Christ. He did not speak as if Israel were lost in

[1] Ezra 7 : 13, 28.

Assyria, only to be discovered as the Anglo-Saxon race in this nineteenth century. Paul, too, before Agrippa, spoke of the "twelve tribes instantly serving God day and night," entirely unconscious that only two tribes were then known to be in existence, according to the modern discoverer. James, also, dedicates his epistle to the "twelve tribes" just as if none were missing. Lastly, the people themselves, on one occasion, cried out, "Men of Israel, help," without the least apparent thought that all Israel were "lost" and hundreds of miles away. In fact, the two divisions in the nation were again united, so that all twelve tribes were known as Israel or as the Jews. Some of the expressions just quoted no doubt refer to the true Israel of God instead of to the Hebrews as a nation, but in either case they are equally to the point in proving that no portion was "lost." In a national sense they were all restored to Judea, and in the spiritual sense they are all treated as one people. Their union, especially in the latter sense, is shown by a symbolic representation, a part of which we quote: —

Moreover, thou son of man, take thee one stick, and write upon it, For Judah, and for the children of Israel his companions: then take another stick, and write upon it, For Joseph, the stick of Ephraim, and for all the house of Israel his companions: *and join them one to another into one stick, and they shall become one in thine hand.* And when the children of thy people shall speak unto thee, saying, Wilt thou not show us what thou meanest by these? say unto them, Thus saith the Lord God; Behold, I will take the stick of Joseph, which is in the hand of Ephraim, and the tribes of Israel his fellows, and will put them with him, even with the stick of Judah, and make them one stick, and they shall be one in mine hand. And the sticks whereon thou writest shall be in thine hand before their eyes. And say unto them, Thus saith the Lord God: Behold, I will take the children of Israel from among the heathen, whither they be gone, and will gather them on every side, and bring them into their own land. *And I will make them one nation* in the land upon the mountains of Israel; and one king shall be king to them all; and they shall be no more two nations, neither shall they be divided into two kingdoms any more at all.[1]

We can therefore study the future history of Israel under one head, instead of keeping up the distinction of Judah and Israel as it existed for a short time. All the curses pronounced on the apostate Jews, or Israel, embrace all the Hebrew nation; and all the blessings to the true Israel pertain equally to the twelve tribes. In the former sense we find the entire nation now included in the Jewish race scattered among the nations of the earth; in the latter sense, all Israel are now included in the righteous who are scattered throughout the world. This brings us to notice another theory, commonly known as the —

RETURN OF THE JEWS.

While perhaps comparatively few people have much faith in the lost-Israel theory, already examined and shown to be inconsistent with reason

---

[1] Eze. 37: 16-28.

THE HEBREW NATION.   35

and contrary to Scripture, there is quite a general belief that the Hebrew nation, represented in the modern Jews, is to be gathered back to Palestine and Jerusalem. It will be found, however, that this is an error, caused in part at least by overlooking the true Israel. The utter impossibility of the Hebrew nation being restored is shown by a forcible illustration and application found in the prophecy of Jeremiah. The prophet was commanded to gather the leaders of the people, and to break in pieces a potter's earthen vessel before their eyes; and say unto them: —

> Thus saith the Lord of Hosts: Even so will I break this people and this city, as one breaketh a potter's vessel, *that cannot be made whole again;* and they shall bury them in Tophet, till there be no place to bury. *Thus will I do unto this place, saith the Lord,* and to the inhabitants thereof and even make this city as Tophet.[1]

It would be difficult to find a picture of a more complete ruin. Not until a shattered earthen bottle can be made whole, need men expect the Hebrew nation to be gathered. This is simply saying that it will never be accomplished. The context clearly shows that the destruction of Jerusalem by the Roman army in A. D. 70 is the one which fulfils this prediction, and that the dispersion of the Jews since that time is the one which will never be changed. It is everywhere evident that all promises made to Israel for the future must refer to the true people of God by that name, and not to the

[1] Jer. 19: 10–12.

Hebrew nation, the literal Jews, nor to any earthly government.

GOD'S PROMISES.

Some people are slow to accept fully the obvious facts here set forth, fearing that in some way the promises of God will fail if the scattered Hebrews are not gathered; but such should remember that truth is not contradictory, and in due time we shall be able to demonstrate that their solicitude is unnecessary. If time and space permitted, it would be a pleasant task to discuss each separate promise; but we must be content merely to present a few general principles, which cover a multitude of particular texts bearing on the subject.

In a majority of cases the application of certain passages is made plain and easy by keeping in mind that there is a true Israel, distinct from any national lines. If this fundamental truth is ignored, only confusion can possibly be the result. The language of the text and the context will show whether it should be understood of any condition in this world, or whether it reaches over into the "world to come," where the earth will be created anew, and the curse of sin removed.

Some scriptures which evidently refer to national Israel, and foretell their return from captivity, had complete fulfilment in the restoration from Assyrian and Babylonian bondage, already discussed in this chapter. All the Old Testament prophets except Malachi uttered their predictions before, or during the time of, the return granted by Cyrus and his successors. Hence the chronology of these promises would not be inconsistent with such application. Some promises of favor and some warnings of wrath were given to them also, which met their fulfilment in the land of Judea, after the restoration and before their final rejection as a nation in the early years of the Christian era.

If, perchance, there are other promises not included in any of these divisions, we must remember that they were given subject to conditions on the part of the people which were not carried out, and therefore were made void by unbelief and disobedience. On this point the following rule is given in the words of the Lord, addressed directly to the Hebrew people under the name of Israel : —

Behold, as the clay is in the potter's hand, so are ye in mine hand, O house of Israel. At what instant I shall speak concerning a nation, and concerning a kingdom, to pluck up, and to pull down, and to destroy it; if that nation, against whom I have pronounced, turn from their evil, I will repent of the evil that I thought to do unto them. And at what instant I shall speak concerning a nation, and concerning a kingdom, to build and to plant it; if it do evil in my sight, that it obey not my voice, then I will repent of the good, wherewith I said I would benefit them. Now therefore go to, speak to the men of Judah, and to the inhabitants of Jerusalem, saying, Thus saith the Lord: Behold, I frame evil against you, and devise a device against you; return ye now every one from his evil way, and make your ways and your doings good. And they said, There is no hope; but we will walk after our own devices, and we will every one do the imagination of his evil heart.[1]

In the face of these words, and in view of the continued and proverbial stubbornness of that people, who can now assert that God is under obligation to restore them to their former place and position?

CONVERSION OF THE JEWS.

But it may be urged further that the Jews, now scattered in unbelief, will yet turn to the Lord and be converted, so that they can be restored. If this were really so, they would then be *true Israelites*, and of course entitled to the same blessings that all the righteous will receive. Our argument would not be changed at all in that case; for we contend that converted persons of all nations constitute the Israel of God, but that nothing comes to men who abide still in unbelief because of any national distinction.

The supposition, however, has no foundation; it is not true that all the Jews will be converted. That some of this ancient race will receive the gospel, we may be sure; but where is the evidence that practically all, or even a majority, of them will be converted? After 1800 years in opposition to Christ, are they now more inclined than other men to confess the true Messiah? Judging from past results, what are the prospects for the future in this direction? God has no other gospel for them; there is no other Holy Spirit to convince of

[1] Jer. 18:6-12.

sin, righteousness, and judgment to come; there are no new Scriptures; there is no time more favorable than the present, and yet how few receive the message now. Facts are stubborn things to array against a cherished theory; but the man who loves truth will gladly forsake any position opposed to Scripture, and contrary to common experience and observation.

We do not deny that a great many Jews, and other people, too, may yet return to Palestine, *expecting* that a new nation of Israel is to be formed under the dominion of Christ on David's throne. A world-wide sentiment is developing in that direction, and a corresponding movement will doubtless soon begin; but let it be distinctly understood that the *Lord* is not leading in such an enterprise; it is not in accordance with his plans, and it will end in disaster to all who are deceived by it. Therefore even if all the Jews in the world, and many Gentiles, should yet migrate to Judea, it would not in the least prove that they are correct in their anticipations; nor would it disprove the facts presented to the contrary in this book. Our argument is not based on the course men may choose to follow, but, rather, on what the Scriptures teach in the matter.

AN IMPRESSIVE LESSON.

Those who contend that in the future special blessings pertain to the national Israel, will do well to mark the ruin which a similar idea brought upon the nation of Israel in the past. The Jews of old made the same mistake that many so-called Christians are repeating to-day; namely, they thought the mere fact that they were descended from Abraham gave them a right to claim all the divine favor promised to his "seed." Self-righteousness and national pride resulted; and instead of their manifesting the lovely disposition of the children of God, they became noted for selfish cruelty toward one another and contemptuous arrogance toward people of other nations. The Lord sent his servants, and finally his Son, in order that they might learn what true Israel means; but they despised the prophets and killed the Saviour. At last the Lord destroyed the nation, so that all men might see that no hope can be placed on that. He shattered the idol they worshiped that they and others might turn to the Lord for a humble, contrite heart.

John the Baptist warned the unconverted Jewish teachers that they should not say in their hearts, "We have Abraham to our father" while their fruits were evil, and reminded them that God would, if necessary, raise up other people out of the stones, in order that only righteous persons should be numbered with true Israel. Christ, too, plainly told those who were seeking to slay him that they were not children of Abraham. Paul also, even after their rejection by the Lord, labored to convince them that national birth did not entitle them to any special privileges

After thus impressively showing that only ruin could follow trust in men, what shall be said for those zealous, but misguided, modern teachers who again expect a restoration of Israel as a nation, with special blessings, simply because they were born of Hebrew parents? Is God now leading people to believe the very thing which brought destruction eighteen centuries ago? Will the false hope which caused their ruin then, save those who believe it in these days? Rather, is not history about to be repeated? and will not those who pin their faith to theories of Israel's superiority as a nation, be caught hopelessly and eternally in the enemy's snare?

CONCLUSIONS FROM THE FOREGOING.

The reader will please observe the harmony thus far found on these points. In Chapter I it was shown that all future blessings were for true Israel in distinction from the nation sometimes called by the name "Israel." In this chapter we arrive at the same conclusion by an opposite course. Tracing the national history, we find no promise that the Hebrews will ever be restored, but direct testimony to the contrary. Thus, from whichever direction the subject is independently studied, the conclusions are the same. This part of the Eastern Question is answered. The Lord will never gather the Jews back to the so-called Holy Land.

Equally conclusive results have been reached

condemning what is called the Anglo-Israel theory. The Lord has not commissioned any nation or people to reconquer the land of Judea and establish a kingdom at Jerusalem. All the Lord's promises to be fulfilled in the future belong to the true Israel, and in succeeding chapters we shall learn in what way they are connected with the Eastern Question. All we need to say now is that true Israel will take no part in the warlike struggle. The weapons of their warfare are not carnal. Their message is the gospel of peace unto all men. "Love your enemies" is their motto. "Whatsoever ye would that men should do to you, do ye even so to them," is their rule of life. Their voices will not be heard in the clamor for the "Christian nations" to drive out the Turk; for their Master has said, "All they that take the sword shall perish with the sword." The meek and lowly Christ healing the wounded ear that had been cut off by a rash disciple, is the pattern for true Israel to-day. He, while hanging on the cross, was the true "King of Israel," but the world knew him not. The world knows not his followers to-day. They are lost in the eyes of men, branded as heretics, punished as criminals, and despised for faithful adherence to the commandments of God and the faith of Jesus. They are "princes of God," Israelites indeed; but they receive not the honor of men. They sit not in the lofty seats of human pride and power; and yet they are "heirs of God, and joint heirs with Jesus Christ." There is no danger nor hope that they will be "discovered" for the "lost Israel." A Barabbas would still be saved, and a Christ crucified, by the ambitious multitude claiming to be "lost Israel," but more anxious to have the kingdom of God established at Jerusalem than in their own hearts.

Chapter Three.

THE GENTILE NATIONS.

IN the previous chapters we have briefly traced the true Israel of God, composed of converted individuals out of all nations; also the history of the Hebrews to the time of their final apostasy as a nation, and consequent rejection by the Lord. An understanding of these points prepares us to enter upon the third great division of our subject, by asking, In what way are the Gentile nations connected with the promises to Israel, and thus to the Eastern Question?

First of all, we must understand the absolute equality of all men before the Lord. With him there is no caste, no aristocracy; he has no favorites. The world is slow to recognize this great principle. Notwithstanding the positive assertion of the Bible that "God is no respecter of persons," many still think there must be some difference at least in the time and manner for God to manifest his grace to the diverse portions of the human race. In other words, a common opinion is held that in a past age the Lord favored the Hebrews, while less regard was given to the Gentiles; that in the present age the Gentiles are specially chosen, while the Jews are passed by to a great degree; and that in a future age the Jews will again be restored to pre-eminence, and through them the mass of the Gentiles, still unconverted, will be greatly blessed.

The mere statement of such a changeable policy should lead men to mistrust that it does not emanate from that Being who is without "variableness, neither shadow of turning." His wisdom and goodness would be put in doubt, if such apparently capricious moods were a part of the divine plans. To be perfectly sure that to him there is no actual difference, we will read exact Scripture language on this point: "Is he the God of the Jews only? is he not also of the Gentiles? Yes, of the Gentiles also; seeing it is one God, which shall justify the circumcision by faith, and uncircumcision through faith." "For there is no difference between the Jew and the Greek; for the same Lord over all is rich unto all that call upon him."[1]

This is not the statement of a new policy on the part of the Lord when the New Testament was written. All men are always exactly equal in his favor. Some may learn this truth before it comes to others; but this does not alter the fact that all are invited at the same time, and on the same terms. As soon as one comes to that knowledge, the Lord bids him tell others. No nation and no person has the least reason to claim superior goodness as the first recipients of the gospel. On the contrary, it is a cause for deep humility; for the

[1] Rom. 3:29, 30; 10:12.

Lord says that he uses the weakest and most foolish men to proclaim the gospel; "not many wise men after the flesh, not many mighty, not many noble, are called." Just as soon as men or nations get the idea that they are superior to other men, they cannot preach the true gospel at all. Much pride and vain boasting would be avoided if this truth were duly recognized.

THE CALL OF ABRAHAM.

Abraham was born and reared in heathen darkness. His parents and companions were idolaters. He had done no good works by which to merit the favor of God. In some way the Lord's grace for sinners was made known to him, and he believed it. By that faith he was made righteous, and he was called the "Friend of God." But there were many other heathen men; and the Lord gave the gospel to him to carry to others, so that they too might come in the same way. He was a missionary to the heathen: "And the Scripture, foreseeing that God would justify the heathen through faith, preached before the gospel unto Abraham, saying, *In thee shall all nations be blessed.* So then they which be of faith are blessed with faithful Abraham."[1] In calling this man to separate from all his heathen kindred and go out as a teacher of righteousness, the Lord said: "*In thee shall all families of the earth be blessed.*" Other nations were not forgotten nor neglected in this early work

[1] Gal. 3 : 8, 9.

of the gospel. Abraham alone could not do all the gracious work the Lord was waiting to accomplish; therefore the additional promise of a numerous posterity for the same purpose was given: "And I will make of thee a *great nation*, and I will bless thee, and make thy name great; *and thou shalt be a blessing.*"[1]

THE CALL OF ISRAEL.

At once it will be seen that only those who had the character of Abraham could really impart his blessing to others. Selfish, proud persons could not properly represent the Lord, who is meek and lowly in heart. Only a few of Abraham's posterity had that disposition; the Hebrews as a nation were a stubborn, rebellious people. Only a few of the great multitude delivered from Egypt were Israelites indeed. Paul writes concerning their experience in the wilderness as follows: "For unto us was the gospel preached, as well as unto them; but the word preached did not profit them, not being mixed with faith in them that heard it."[2] It was God's purpose to use them to show his grace to all the world; but instead of recognizing this fact and permitting his Spirit to mold their lives, they murmured and rebelled at each lesson he gave. Their posterity who finally entered the promised land were of the same character. A few out of each generation were truly Israelites, but the majority were proud and stubborn. They were called to be missionaries to the world — a people so lovable and

[1] Gen. 12: 2, 3. [2] Heb. 4: 2.

wise that other nations would be led to know and love the God of Israel; but they interpreted the grace of God to them as evidence that they were much better than others, and so became self-righteous and overbearing toward those less highly favored. Moses set the matter before them in the true light: —

> Understand therefore, that the Lord thy God giveth thee not this good land to possess it for thy righteousness; for thou art a stiffnecked people.[1] Behold, I have taught you statutes and judgments, even as the Lord my God commanded me, that ye should do so in the land whither ye go to possess it. Keep therefore and do them; for this is your wisdom and your understanding in the sight of the nations, which shall hear all these statutes, and say, Surely this great nation is a wise and understanding people. For what nation is there so great, who hath God so nigh unto them, as the Lord our God is in all things that we call upon him for? And what nation is there so great, that hath statutes and judgments so righteous as all this law, which I set before you?[2]

God promised that his holy presence should separate them from all other people in character; but he did not intend that they should shut themselves away from the rest of the world, so that they could not proclaim the gospel. The Lord was not indifferent to the rest of the world; but the people he had chosen to publish his name did not respond to his call. They were not all Israel which were of Israel. As they lost the presence of God by their continued apostasy, artificial rules and creeds

---

[1] Deut. 9:6.   [2] Deut. 4:5-8.

were invented to keep up an outward show of separation, until at last it became unlawful in their estimation to mingle with their Gentile neighbors, or even speak to them. How could such a people be the light of the world and the salt of the earth? How could the Gentile nations learn the gospel from such an unlovely nation?

At last the time of their visitation came, and they knew it not. A greater than Abraham was with them. The King of Israel was on earth, doing the very work of a true Israelite; but so different was he from their standard that he was not recognized by them. He was a servant of men and the "friend of sinners." In sorrow the Messiah wept over their sins and their coming doom. He had been a husband to them during all the long centuries of their wantonness; in all their afflictions he was afflicted; but nothing could win their love. Finally they chose a murderer, and killed the Prince of Life, while calling for his blood to rest upon them and their children forever. The blow soon fell, and the unbelieving branches were broken off and scattered.

INDIVIDUAL SALVATION.

While apostate Israel were thus cast away as a nation, individuals were still invited to believe and be grafted back into the good olive-tree. Their "blindness" was only in "part." They had not stumbled that they should fall without hope. God forbid. As a nation, their hope was shattered; but they could still be connected with the true Israel through faith. Paul refers to his own conversion, as "one born out of due time," to prove this point. "I say then, Hath God cast away his people? God forbid. For I also am an Israelite, of the seed of Abraham, of the tribe of Benjamin. God hath not cast away his people which he foreknew."[1] The unbelief of those who had been cast away, could not make the promise of God to the true Israel of none effect. Repentant Jews are just as acceptable as repentant Gentiles, and Paul labored "if by any means" he "might save some of them."

THE GENTILES CALLED.

The fall of national Israel brought riches to the world. The gospel could now be made known to the Gentiles, so that they might share in the blessings of Abraham and true Israel. It was not a new gospel on different conditions; but it was the same old gospel which for centuries the Lord had desired them to learn from what he could do through the Hebrew nation. All the while he had waited to bless all the nations with the blessing of Abraham, but the perversity of Israel had hindered this design. Now it had come to them by the removal of the nation which had selfishly stood in the way. God does not save the Jews by the law, and Gentiles by the gospel. There is not a particle of difference between them. Every moral obligation

[1] Rom. 11: 1, 2.

given to Israel is to be recognized by true Israel to-day. The commandments of God and the faith of Jesus go hand in hand throughout all ages.

In these days careless persons think that the Gentiles enjoy many more privileges and much greater liberty than pertained to Israel. Some even boast that they are Gentiles, and therefore not under obligation to keep the ten commandments. They seem to think that the old covenant was made with Israel, and that the new covenant is made with the Gentiles. This is a grave mistake. Both covenants — the new as well as the old — were made with Israel. No covenant has ever been made with the Gentiles. Moreover, the same law is the basis of both covenants, and the same gospel is connected with both. This will be seen clearly by the following quotation: —

> For if that first covenant had been faultless, then should no place have been sought for the second. For finding fault with them, he saith, Behold, the days come, saith the Lord, when I will make a new covenant with the *house of Israel* and with the *house of Judah.* . . . For this is the covenant that I will make with the house of Israel after those days, saith the Lord: I will put my laws into their mind, and write them in their hearts; and I will be to them a God, and they shall be to me a people.[1]

Here we learn that the new covenant was made with Israel, not with the Gentiles. The same great truth is expressed in Rom. 9:4, where Paul mentions the things which pertain to Israel; namely,

[1] Heb. 8:8-10.

the adoption, the glory, the *covenants*, the giving of the law, the service of God, and the promises. Instead of the Gentiles having more than Israel, they have absolutely nothing, while Israel has all. God has not removed the blessings from Israel, nor granted others to the Gentiles; but the whole plan of the gospel, first, last, and all the time, is to call Gentiles unto the blessings in store for Israel. And right here is the blessed fact that Israel is not limited to one nation, but that any person who accepts Christ as king in his own heart is entitled to all the privileges of the kingdom of God. Israel is still the chosen people. God has not cast away the people whom he foreknew. The fall of the Hebrew nation did not change his plan a particle. True Israel has always included every converted person of all nations, and no one else. A Gentile, in God's sight, is simply an unrepentant sinner, and an Israelite is a repentant saint. Paul sets forth the miserable condition of all Gentiles as follows: —

Wherefore remember, that ye being in time past Gentiles in the flesh, . . . that at that time ye were without Christ, being aliens from the commonwealth of Israel, and strangers from the covenants of promise, having no hope, and without God in the world.[1]

A more melancholy situation cannot be described. Under the provisions of the new covenant, there is not a particle of hope for any Gentile who does not become a true Israelite. "Salvation is of the

[1] Eph. 2: 11, 12.

Jews," said Christ — not of those who are Jews outwardly, but those who are Jews inwardly. No covenant is made with Gentiles; no Christ is their Saviour; they have no hope in God. All these belong to Israel, and Israel is all who come to Christ.

CHRISTIANS.

True Israelites are exactly identical with true Christians. It is only by becoming Christ's that anybody can be Abraham's seed. But it is well to emphasize the point that the promises of the Bible are made to all the people of God under the name of "Israel" instead of "Christians." Strictly speaking, there is no such thing as a "Gentile Christian;" for a Gentile is without Christ, and therefore cannot be a Christian. When a person is converted, he is no more a Gentile, but an Israelite. In no case is it proper to contrast the moral character or requirements of a true Christian and a true Israelite; for they are the same. The Old Testament is for Christians as well as Israelites, and the New Testament is for Israelites as well as Christians. The two names are identical in both cases. The true Christian is simply a true Israelite manifested, and the New Testament is simply the Old Testament revealed. The gospel in both is simply the law in Christ. The covenant made with Abraham is identical with the new covenant ratified with the blood of Christ.

God is no respecter of persons. "If ye be Christ's, then are ye Abraham's seed, and heirs according to the promise."[1] Outside of Christ and of connection with the commonwealth of Israel, there is no promise to any person. It is not a mere Christian profession, but a Christian character, that constitutes a true Israelite. The great mass of the Hebrew nation were not Israelites, and the great majority in so-called "Christian nations" are not Christians. "If any man have not the Spirit of Christ, he is none of his." Certain church forms will no more save persons to-day than the ancient Jewish forms and ceremonies would save individuals in a past age. A few then really understood the gospel. Caleb and Joshua among the multitude who left Egypt; seven thousand who had not bowed the knee to Baal in the time of Elijah; and a "remnant according to the election of grace" in the time of Paul, are samples of the "little flock" in each generation who now compass us "about with so great a cloud of witnesses." The same relative proportion are true Christians to-day — a few in each generation and in each nation, but in the final aggregate constituting, with their companions of the ancient faith, "a great multitude which no man could number." Let no one suppose that the coming of Christ into the world has changed the moral law, so that transgression of any commandment is no longer sin. True faith in Christ will still be manifested by obedience to all

---

[1] Gal. 3 : 29.

the commandments of God; and self-righteousness is still shown by exalting the traditions and forms of the church "fathers" above the precepts of the divine law.

BOASTING PROHIBITED.

Due consideration of the foregoing facts will prepare us to understand the warning of Paul against Gentile boasting. After setting forth the matter that the fall of national Israel had opened the way for the Gentiles to share in the fulness of true Israel, through the gospel, he says: —

> Boast not against the branches. But if thou boast, thou bearest not the root, but the root thee. Thou wilt say then, The branches were broken off, that I might be grafted in. Well; because of unbelief they were broken off, and thou standest by faith. Be not high-minded, but fear. For if God spared not the natural branches, take heed lest he also spare not thee. Behold therefore the goodness and severity of God; on them which fell severity; but toward thee, goodness, if thou continue in his goodness; otherwise thou also shalt be cut off. . . . For I would not, brethren, that ye should be ignorant of this mystery, lest ye should be wise in your own conceits; that blindness in part is happened to Israel, until the fulness of the Gentiles be come in.[1]

It will be well to spend a moment longer on these words of caution. Here the apostle shows the only method by which any person, whether Jew or Gentile, can become an Israelite. He is not one by nature, but he must be grafted into the good olive-tree *contrary to nature.* The Jew cannot claim the pre-eminence, and the Gentile cannot

[1] Rom. 11 : 18-25.

boast; for both alike are without hope until they in the same manner receive Christ by a new birth, and thus become true Israelites.

ALL ISRAEL TO BE SAVED.

Having thus shown us that there is no difference in the time or way of saving Jews or Gentiles who abide not still in unbelief, but that by faith all may alike be grafted into the good olive-tree, the apostle now reaches the climax of his argument with the triumphant conclusion, "*And so all Israel shall be saved.*" Yes; this is the true Israel which through all ages God has been calling. It makes no difference what their nation may be; but they have accepted the gospel in Christ, and so all Israel will at last be made up and saved.

Strangely enough, this text is often misunderstood to teach that the Jews, or Israel, as a nation according to the flesh, are yet to be saved; but this is not the case, as we have already learned from other scriptures, and it is contrary to the discourse of Paul in this chapter. He was endeavoring to prove that unbelieving Jews who had been broken off, and the Gentiles who had never been connected with God's people, were in precisely the same condition. Neither could boast; for both must be grafted in contrary to nature and stand by faith. Now the apostle does not turn about and contradict all his former statements, by asserting, as some suppose, that the Jews are at present excluded to some degree from the gospel, and that in a future age they will all be saved. He has his mind on true Israel, and he shows how God is making up his chosen people even though the Hebrews as a nation had been rejected forever. By all the world having the opportunity to hear the gospel, and some of each nation accepting it, the number will at last be reached, and *so* all Israel shall be saved.

The adverb "*so*" relates to *manner*, but not to *time*. Paul does not say that the fulness of the Gentiles must first come, and that *afterward* all Israel will be saved. Nothing is affirmed of a future age. He simply shows a certain method which God employs for accomplishing his purpose, and then states that "*so*" — by that means — "all Israel shall be saved."

BLINDNESS TO ISRAEL.

But it may be objected that the apostle speaks of the literal Hebrews as being blinded at the present time, so that they cannot come to God on the same terms as the Gentiles. But we reply, Paul certainly knew how to construct a consistent argument; and after so many times asserting that there is no difference between the Jews and the Gentiles, he does not here declare that there is a difference by which some are prevented while others are assisted. The blindness of the Jews is not a divine infliction upon them, but it is caused by their own unbelief. The rejection of God's truth will always cause spiritual blindness. Pharaoh's heart was hardened, or he was blinded, in the same way. God showed him his power, but Pharaoh resisted it all. To the Hebrew people God revealed his grace; but they refused to walk in it, and so they were blinded. Paul states the fact, after illustrating it by the veil Moses put over his face to hide the glory which the people could not endure because of their sins: —

But their minds were blinded: for until this day remaineth the same veil untaken away in the reading of the old testament; which veil is done away in Christ. But even unto this day, when Moses is read, the veil is upon their heart. Nevertheless when it [the heart] shall turn to the Lord, the veil shall be taken away.[1]

Satan, the god of this world, is the one who "hath blinded the minds of them which believe not." God has never interposed to darken the minds of the Jews, or of any one else; but he seeks to let light shine upon all men at all times to the fullest degree that they will receive it. There is no reason in the world why any Jew or any Gentile is blinded, except by his own unbelief.

Notice further that the blindness mentioned by Paul is only in "part." The Jews as a nation have fallen forever; but as individuals they still stand on precisely the same terms as the Gentiles. The gospel to-day is for them the same as for other men, and a few of them, "by abiding not still in

[1] 2 Cor. 3: 14–16.

unbelief," are changed to Israelites indeed. But the question may be asked, Does not the language of Paul imply that when the fulness of the Gentiles is come in, the "blindness in part" will be done away, so that in a future age they will be converted?— No, it does not imply that; but it does imply that their partial blindness will become *total darkness.* Now there is hope; but then everlasting oblivion will be the consequence of their continued unbelief. All Israel will be saved when the fulness of the Gentiles is come in, and there will be no further proclamation of the gospel; hence the blindness will be total and perpetual instead of less. "Now is the accepted time; behold, now is the day of salvation."

THE GENTILE FULNESS.

What is meant by the "fulness of the Gentiles"? Before giving a direct answer, we will notice the fulness of nations in the past. The Lord said to Abraham concerning his seed who should be in bondage: "But in the fourth generation they shall come hither again; for the iniquity of the Amorites is not yet full."[1] The Amorites were one of the nations of Canaan; but the Lord would not permit them to be driven out immediately, for their iniquity was not yet full. Their fulness was a fulness of sin. For four hundred years the Lord sought to redeem them, after the promise to Abraham was made; but at last their cup of guilt was full. They

[1] Gen. 15:16.

would not repent; their probation ended, and they were destroyed.

The same principle applies to the antediluvians. Their wickedness was great; but the Lord extended their probation for one hundred and twenty years, in order that the message of Noah might be proclaimed to them. By the Holy Spirit, Christ preached to those spirits in prison, "while the ark was a preparing, when once the long-suffering of God waited in the days of Noah."[1] At the end of this period, their sin had increased until there was no further hope of repentance. "And God saw that the wickedness of man was great in the earth, and that every imagination of the thoughts of his heart was only evil continually."[2] They rejected the gospel, going deeper into sinful pleasure and violence, until their fulness came, and the flood swept them away.

For nearly fifteen hundred years the Lord sought to save the Hebrew nation, by sending them prophets, and finally his own Son. John the Baptist pointed out the doom of the nation unless they should repent, and receive the One who stood among them as the Lamb of God. But all was in vain, so far as the mass of the people were concerned. Christ wept over their coming doom, and pointed out that they were no better than their fathers, who had killed the prophets; and the final word was, "*Fill ye up then the measure* of your fathers." While their day of hope was

---

[1] 1 Peter 3: 20.   [2] Gen. 6: 5.

about to pass, they filled up the terrible cup by crucifying their King, and rejecting the preaching of his apostles. This was the "fulness" of that nation, and the Roman armies destroyed their city, and scattered them forever.

From these instances we may learn what is meant by the "fulness of the Gentiles," yet to come. For more than eighteen hundred years the gospel message has sounded in the ears of the Gentile world, and they have had the history of the past, which has been written for their benefit. To each individual who knows the grace of God the message is given to say to others still in darkness, "Come." Each Christian is to be a living epistle, known and read by all men. The very love of God to the sinful race will be manifested by them even to the most vicious and degraded of men. All honor to the faithful men and women who have upheld the true gospel at home and abroad. They are Israelites indeed. But, alas! many who bear the name of Christ do not truly represent him before the world. War is the science of the age; and so-called "Christian nations" are now foremost in using carnal weapons. When representatives from heathen countries visit our shores, they learn the art of war instead of the gospel of peace we profess. When we go abroad in heathen lands, it is for conquest and selfish trade. Rum and ruin are carried to the savage tribes. If, perchance, our converts and missionaries are persecuted and killed, how quickly the military power is sent to shoot their enemies. Among the civilized nations, jealousy and treachery pass for patriotism. What kind of gospel are we carrying to the world? Are we better than ancient Israel?

It is this spirit of strife which is urging on the Eastern Question, and all the signs of the times will fail if a war of tremendous magnitude is not the result. When it comes, what will be the effect? Is the "fulness of the Gentiles" about come in? and is the gathering storm of divine wrath about to break? These are momentous questions. We will not attempt to answer them fully now, but following pages will bring us to the subject again. For the present let it suffice to say that the "fulness of the Gentiles" will bring the close of all earthly hopes, the end of the gospel, and the saving of all Israel. God will once more send the knowledge of his truth to all the world, as he did by Noah and John in past times. True Israel will thus be made up, and the Gentiles who refuse the light will be left in total darkness and ruin. No future age of salvation is to come, but a little more time is left before the present day of peace is gone. Now is the time to learn the real meaning of the term "Israel of God," and the significance to them and to all the world of the Eastern Question.

REMARKS.

In concluding this chapter we will merely call attention again to the harmony and beauty of the subjects thus far considered. When the true Israel is recognized, there is a golden thread running all through the Bible. God's plan is understood in his dealings with the nations and with individuals. Everything centers in Israel, for Christ is king in their hearts and lives. The destiny of the world is waiting for them to be sought out. Only confusion and disappointment await those who look for a future age of grace for either Jew or Gentile. Just how much longer it will take for the fulness of salvation to come for all Israel, and the fulness of destruction for the Gentiles, no one can tell; but it may be near. At any rate the Eastern Question hangs over the world with ominous darkness, and the issue cannot long be deferred. Meanwhile the nations go on perfecting the deadliest implements for slaughtering men. What will be the end of all these things?

Chapter Four.

THE HEATHEN NATIONS.

THUS far our argument has embraced three great divisions of the human family,—true Israel, including all the righteous of every age and nation; the Hebrew people, for a time called Israel in a restricted sense; and the Gentile nations, which are composed of unconverted men of all ages. Again, some who have formerly been only Hebrews or Gentiles, become Israelites indeed, without changing their national distinction. In other words, natural relationships, either family or national, are not altered by the acceptance of Christ, and adoption into the Israel of God; neither is any one entitled to a place among the chosen of God because of any earthly connection. Only divine power can beget true Israelites; but the precious privilege of being reckoned among the Israel of God is bestowed with absolute impartiality upon all who, like Jacob, prevail with God by faith.

These principles are so consistent and Scriptural that it is a marvel that so many practically deny them by insisting that the literal Jews and the various Gentile nations are the subjects of future promises, ignoring, to a great degree, the claims of the very class called the "Israel of God" in the Bible. To apply to the same identical Israel, the denunciations of divine wrath and the promises of divine favor, is not only illogical, but it involves an accusation against the perfect truthfulness of God. Who can honestly suppose that when the Lord says, "For I will no more have mercy upon the house of Israel; but I will utterly take them away," he means the same persons who are mentioned in immediate connection, "Yet the number of the children of Israel shall be as the sand of the sea, which cannot be measured nor numbered; and it shall come to pass, that in the place where it was said unto them, Ye are not my people, there it shall be said unto them, Ye are the sons of the living God. Then shall the children of Judah and the children of Israel be gathered together, and appoint themselves one head, and they shall come up out of the land."[1] This is a sample of many contradictions, if only a national Israel is recognized; but there is harmony when the true Israel is placed in contrast with the rebellious literal seed.

Only one additional division of the race demands notice, but this, in point of numbers, far surpasses all the others combined. What about the heathen nations? How will God deal with the millions of each generation who have not enjoyed the full gospel light? This has been a difficult

[1] Hosea 1:7-11.

problem to theologians. The common view, which assigns this vast host to endless misery, is too horrible for belief. To avoid this dreadful libel on God's character of love and justice, the theory of a future probation has been invented. Its advocates usually admit that the Scriptures do not directly express such an idea; but as the only alternative to the former doctrine, they boldly endorse it, with the hope that it may prove to be correct. This hypothesis is generally connected in some way with the supposed restoration of the Jews and the ultimate salvation of the Gentiles, in an age subsequent to the present day of grace.

The Eastern Question is considered as inseparably associated with the opening of the millennium, when all these changes will occur. One by one we will examine each of these points. Already we have discovered that the so-called restoration of the Jews is a fable; also that Gentiles who remain without Christ are still without hope, and that when their "fulness is come in" at the close of the present age, their probation will close forever; and lastly, that true Israel will all be saved by the present plan of grafting in Jew and Gentile. Consequently there can be no further period of salvation necessary or possible, except for the heathen. Are they an exception to the rest of mankind? If not, then the theory of a future gospel age is entirely disproved by showing that no necessity exists for it. But in this case how can the impartiality of

God be manifested? To this main question we now ask the reader's attention.

That "God is no respecter of persons" is an established fact. Therefore he will deal with the people in heathen lands precisely as he deals with individuals in more favored lands. God's invariable rule is that each person is accountable only for the opportunities he has. Some have much more light than others; but faithfulness to the little is counted as acceptable as faithfulness to greater light. This principle is illustrated in the parable of the talents. The man who doubled his two talents received the same commendation as the one who doubled his five. Proportionately to the amount received in each case, there was no difference in the result. In plain language the same rule is elsewhere stated as follows:—

And that servant, which knew his Lord's will, and prepared not himself, neither did according to his will, shall be beaten with many stripes. But he that knew not, and did commit things worthy of stripes, shall be beaten with few stripes. For unto whomsoever much is given, of him shall be much required.[1] He that is faithful in that which is least is faithful also in much: and he that is unjust in the least is unjust also in much.[2]

No one can deny that absolute justice is here set forth. Neither more nor less can be required. Under this divine measurement, the poor heathen in Africa or India stand on precisely the same footing as the most civilized people of other lands.

While the light is less in the former case, the responsibility also is less in the same degree. One single ray of light, faithfully followed, will lead to the Source of light — Jesus Christ, the Sun of Righteousness; and any portion of light rejected will result in total darkness. Hear how the Lord expresses this truth: —

And this is the condemnation, that light is come into the world, and men loved darkness rather than light, because their deeds were evil. For every one that doeth evil hateth the light, neither cometh to the light, lest his deeds should be reproved. But he that doeth truth cometh to the light, that his deeds may be made manifest, that they are wrought in God.[1] If I had not come and spoken unto them, they had not had sin; but now they have no cloak for their sin.[2]

Who can say but that in the eyes of an impartial Judge some at least of the so-called heathen have walked more faithfully in their dim light from heaven, than have many nominal Christians in the flood of light shining on their track? No doubt on this point can exist in the face of the words of Christ which follow: —

Then began he to upbraid the cities wherein most of his mighty works were done, because they repented not: Woe unto thee Chorazin! woe unto thee Bethsaida! for if the mighty works, which were done in you, had been done in Tyre and Sidon, they would have repented long ago in sackcloth and ashes. But I say unto you, It shall be more tolerable for Tyre and Sidon at the day of judgment, than for you. And thou, Capernaum, which art exalted unto heaven, shalt be brought down to hell: for if the mighty works,

[1] John 3: 19–21.   [2] John 15: 22.

which have been done in thee, had been done in Sodom, it would have remained until this day. But I say unto you, that it shall be more tolerable for the land of Sodom in the day of judgment than for thee.[1]

Of course it does not follow from the foregoing that all the heathen have walked in the little light and truth they knew, any more than that those more privileged have been true to all their greater blessings. Comparatively few of either class have cherished the light which revealed their special sins. But there is no more occasion to grant another period of probation to the most darkened heathen, than there is to grant a similar time to the most enlightened professors of Christianity who have rejected truth from God. No one but the great Searcher of hearts can tell how many have improved the talents committed to their use; but may we not entertain a Scriptural hope that many of all nations, kindreds, tongues, and peoples will stand with the redeemed throng? When Christ separates the sheep from the goats, some will be found at his right hand who have had no expectation of such an honor, while on the other hand will be many who have said, "Lord, Lord," but are not recognized as his people. The despised publicans and harlots, having accepted the grace of Christ and been purified thereby, will go into the kingdom, while the self-righteous Pharisee, depending on his own merits, will be shut out.

[1] Matt. 11 : 20-24.

THE GOSPEL IN NATURE.

To some degree the gospel of Christ has been made known to every intelligent human being that ever lived. It is true that some have not had access to the printed Scriptures. They have never seen a missionary or heard the name of Christ pronounced by mortal lips; and yet they have heard the voice of God speaking to their hearts; they have read his words on tables of stone, and seen his glory in the works of his hand. Notice how distinctly this truth is stated in the Bible: —

> The heavens declare the glory of God; and the firmament showeth his handiwork. Day unto day uttereth speech, and night unto night showeth knowledge. There is no speech nor language, where their voice is not heard. Their line is gone out through all the earth, and their words to the end of the world. In them hath he set a tabernacle for the sun.[1]

Here are preachers of righteousness that go to every person under the canopy of heaven. He who has stood under the blue dome of the sky, surrounded by the green fields, the gray rocks, or the dense, dark forests, has been in God's mission chapel, and heard the still small voice of the Almighty. We know these words of God are correctly applied; for the Holy Spirit through Paul has quoted them to show that the gospel has gone to all the world: —

> But they have not all obeyed the gospel. For Esaias saith, Lord, who hath believed our report? So then faith

[1] Ps. 19: 1-4.

cometh by hearing, and hearing by the word of God. *But I say, Have they not heard? Yes verily, their sound went into all the earth, and their words unto the ends of the world.*[1]

Paul states the purpose of God in creation, and tells why the mass of mankind are still in such gross darkness, notwithstanding his grace manifested to them by his constant care through the operations of nature: —

Because that which may be known of God is manifest in them; for God hath showed it unto them. For the invisible things of him from the creation of the world are clearly seen, being understood by the things that are made, even his eternal power and Godhead; *so that they are without excuse:* because that, when they knew God, they glorified him not as God, neither were thankful; but became vain in their imagination, and their foolish heart was darkened. Professing themselves to be wise, they became fools, and changed the glory of the uncorruptible God into an image made like to corruptible man, and to birds, and four-footed beasts, and creeping things.[2]

Notice carefully each point in the foregoing quotations. God has manifested his invisible power to all men by the creation of the world. So clearly is this seen, and so fully is the gospel thus preached, *"that they are without excuse"* who do not recognize the true God. Once they knew him; but they did not walk in his light, and so "their foolish heart was darkened." The Sabbath was instituted in the beginning of the world to be a constant memorial of the true God revealed in creation; but

---

[1] Rom. 10: 16–18.   [2] Rom. 1: 19–23.

men became so wise in their own imagination that they lost sight of the true character of this gift to the race, and so they forgot God. Objects in nature were then worshiped instead of the One who had created nature. The sun, moon, and various heavenly bodies were first honored; then birds; next four-footed beasts; and lastly creeping things.

In order that Israel might be kept in the knowledge of the true God, the Sabbath was again made known and enjoined upon them; but they, too, misconstrued its gracious design, and made it a grievous yoke by their traditions. "Their foolish heart became darkened" also, and thus "blindness in part" happened unto them, the same as it had to the heathen whom they despised. No doubt the same causes will produce the same effect in the experience of the Gentile nations that disregard the truth of God, in order to follow the pagan festivals of their fathers. In short, the darkness comes because men do not walk in the light they receive. "*They are without excuse;*" therefore another age of probation, if granted, would not change their course. When men have disregarded the grace of God until the light once shed upon them becomes darkness, and the very mercy of God is used to justify continuance in sin, a longer period of probation would only increase their guilt and misery.

A future age of probation is not only unnecessary, but it would be a positive curse to those who have neglected the present salvation. These considerations, coupled with the fact that salvation is now freely offered to every person in the world, on the simple condition that he will accept the light which God bestows, whether little or much, will fully justify the Lord in terminating the probation of all the race at the close of the present age of grace. Instead of dreaming of a future age in which the love of God will be revealed, let all men open their eyes to comprehend the exceeding compassion of God in this present age. "Now is the accepted time; behold, now is the day of salvation."

As already pointed out, the rule of God works both ways. While the disregard of divine power in nature leaves men "without excuse," a faithful acceptance of that knowledge will justify men who have not had greater light. This side of the question is again affirmed by the following quotation: —

For when the Gentiles, which have not the law, do by nature the things contained in the law, these, having not the law, are a law unto themselves: which show the work of the law written in their hearts, their conscience also bearing witness, and their thoughts the meanwhile accusing or else excusing one another.[1]

Thus the degree of gospel light received will either condemn or save, and all men of all nations and generations are treated exactly alike, so far as moral accountability is concerned. This view of the matter entirely justifies the dealings of God

[1] Rom. 2: 14, 15.

with all men, past, present, and future, without resorting to the idea of a future age of probation.

We are not advocating salvation without Christ and the gospel; but we do endorse the Bible doctrine that the gospel is taught in creation and through nature to some degree. Furthermore, we must remember that it was Christ himself who created all things, and therefore he is the one directly revealed by the works done in nature. His true name is his *character*, instead of a mere word or title. Men may know his name of love and mercy in their hearts who have never heard the title of Jesus the Christ. The written word reveals him in a clearer light, but not in opposition to the works of his hand. When necessary to serve his purpose, the true missionary will be sent to such as seek for further light, even as Peter to Cornelius, Philip to the eunuch, Christ to the woman of Samaria, Jonah to the city of Ninevah, or Elijah to the widow of Sarepta. God revealed himself to Abraham in his heathen darkness, and in some way his gospel is spoken to the heart of every human being.

Why, then, send missionaries to the heathen? — For the same reason that we have ministers in Christian lands, namely, to declare the love of God and the richly abounding grace of the gospel. Many are ignorant of God's mercy, and therefore hate him. He does not need to be reconciled to them, but they need to be reconciled to him. Tell them of the infinite pity of him who is no respecter of persons. It is the love of Christ which constrains the true missionary. He does not go to the heathen to tell them that God is angry with them because of their sins, and that they cannot be saved without a future probation of greater light; or that they are doomed to eternal misery because they did not have the Bible; but he goes to let them know that even they are included in the covenant made with Abraham and Christ, on precisely the same terms as other men, now and always. Millions of such missionaries are needed, and the gospel has power to reach darkened hearts. Those who know only the fear of endless torment as an incentive to gospel effort have not yet learned Christ. The "goodness of God" leads men to repentance, and "perfect love" casts out all fear. Then let the love of God to sinners be proclaimed, rather than the fear of hell. And it is *now* that God invites all to come. Those who teach a future "better age" in such glowing words, seem to overlook the fact that they thus deny the *present* lovely character of our God.

WHO ARE HEATHEN?

A few words may be said on the Bible use of the word "heathen." The term is without doubt applied to all who know not God. But true knowledge of God and Jesus Christ is the means of securing eternal life.[1] Consequently all persons who have not by faith received the gift of eternal life, do not

1 John 17: 3.

know God as he is, but are heathen in heart. An intellectual acquaintance with God will never save men from the idols of their hearts. Gold may be worshiped in nominal Christian nations as really as it is in heathen lands. In fact, a false mental conception of God's character is as truly idolatry as to bow down to an image of wood or stone. The Bible declares that covetousness is idolatry. From this it will be seen that if an age of future probation were granted to the "heathen," it would necessarily include nearly all the world; for the Scriptures distinctly teach that only a few really know God aright, and worship him in spirit and in truth.

It may also be pointed out that total destruction, and not eternal conscious torment, is the end of those who know not God; therefore the terrible spectacle of everlasting misery to any portion of the human race is avoided without inventing an unscriptural theory of probation after death, or beyond the present age. One text will suffice on this point: —

For the day of the Lord is near upon all the heathen: as thou hast done, it shall be done unto thee: thy reward shall return upon thine own head. For as ye have drunk upon my holy mountain, so shall all the heathen drink continually, yea, they shall drink, and they shall swallow down, *and they shall be as though they had not been*.[1]

Lastly we may observe that the general teaching of the Scripture is opposed to the theory of a future

---

[1] Obadiah 15, 16.

probation to any individual beyond this present life. Death and the close of the present age are clearly set forth as deciding the eternal destiny of all men for good or for evil. A few Bible statements will establish this conclusion against all the speculations of men: —

> When a righteous man turneth away from his righteousness, and committeth iniquity, and *dieth in them; for his iniquity that he hath done shall he die.*[1] Then said Jesus again unto them, I go my way, and ye shall seek me, *and shall die in your sins: whither I go, ye cannot come.*[2] Whatsoever thy hand findeth to do, do it with thy might; for there is no work, nor device, nor knowledge, nor wisdom, in the grave, whither thou goest.[3]

These references, with many more of like import, make it certain that death ends individual probation. He who dies *in* iniquity, *for* his iniquity he must die again. Not a second probation, but a "*second death*," awaits the person who neglects the present probation until overtaken by the first death. Further evidence to show that the probation of all the race will close with the present age will be reserved to another chapter. But enough has already been said to show that the heathen are not an exception to the general rule. According to the light they have already received, they can be either justified or condemned on the same terms granted to other portions of the race. "Barbarian, Scythian," bond or free, are in the same list as Jew and Gentile. All alike are subjects of

[1] Eze. 18 : 26. [2] John 8 : 21. [3] Eze. 9 : 10.

present grace, and all alike are exposed to future wrath.

THOUGHTS ON THE FOREGOING.

Once more the unity of the divine plan appears. In four divisions we have traced the work of grace to all the human race. In four lines the same truth appears. In moral responsibility all men are exactly equal, and God is not a respecter of persons or nations. One gospel is for all men, and all who receive it are true Israel; all who reject it are Gentiles and heathen. With God there is no division of the gospel into different dispensations for different classes of men. The gospel committed to Adam, Noah, Abraham, Christ, and Paul, is the only gospel now and forever. When the present "day of salvation" is ended, the fulness of true Israel will be reached, and "so all Israel shall be saved;" the "fulness of the Gentiles" will also be "come in," including the unbelieving Jews and the heathen. Emphatically, we see that "*now* is the accepted time." Whatever the Eastern Question may involve in the moral purpose of God, it is for all the race of men.

Chapter Five.

UNIVERSAL RESTORATION.

ONE false doctrine opens the way for another; both then demand a third; and so at last, by logical but fatal steps, the unwary traveler is lost in a labyrinth of speculation. On the other hand, one truth, clearly comprehended and faithfully applied, prepares the mind to grasp a second more readily, and then another, until the whole path "shineth more and more unto the perfect day." These principles, acting in contrary directions, are both illustrated in the subject of this book. We have shown the vast difference between the true Israel of God, and the national Israel, rejected and scattered. Those who take these opposite views on this fundamental question, must of course be led to differ widely at each subsequent step. Our entire understanding of the Eastern Question will depend on which one of these doctrines we adopt. Therefore we wish to clear up the matter as fully as possible before we proceed with other divisions of our main subject.

It cannot be denied that the restoration of **national Israel is advocated and believed by a large** number of people. This, however, by no means proves the theory correct. On the contrary, it is evident that these persons are entirely wrong in every argument and conclusion based upon this idea. To show how far the theory misleads, we will say that nothing short of universal restoration for all mankind, and also for Satan and the fallen angels, can possibly be the logical conclusion. No half-way halt can be made on the road when the journey is once begun. We must accept all or nothing. No one can consistently maintain the return of Israel, as generally understood, without granting that Sodom is likewise to be restored; and no one can admit that Sodom is included in the restoration, and then deny the return of Lucifer to his heavenly home, except by an arbitrary distinction both unreasonable and unscriptural. Some "advanced" teachers boldly contend for this broad redemption for all the sinful. Starting with the return of Israel, they are carried logically to include all other sinful nations, and finally to find the same hope for the evil angels, with Satan at their head. We are perfectly willing to say that if the first proposition is admitted, the other is unavoidable. No doubt many who believe the former will deny the latter; but if they can see that both are parts of the same system, we trust that some at least will abandon the initial error; otherwise they will be quite sure ultimately to accept the conclusion which now they repudiate.

Besides direct Scripture testimony on the point, does not common justice demand that all the sinful shall receive impartial treatment? If one nation which has been rejected on account of sin is to be restored, why should not others have the same privilege? And if wicked men are all subjects of future mercy, why should not fallen angels be redeemed? Where can a line of separation be drawn, when once the principle of a second probation is received? The only possible objection to including all classes is that some are more guilty than others. But this is a fatal admission for the theory; for when we turn to the Bible, we have positive proof that Israel was more wicked than Sodom, according to the light each enjoyed. Therefore if Israel is to be restored, no valid reason can be assigned for Sodom to be everlastingly doomed. Furthermore, a direct comparison between the ruin of Sodom and of the evil angels is made, showing that one is equal to the other. Hence the return of Satan's host is assured, in case Israel is taken back.

We will now turn to the book of Jude, and read the statements about Sodom and fallen angels: —

> And the angels which kept not their first estate, but left their own habitation, he hath reserved in everlasting chains under darkness unto the judgment of the great day. *Even as Sodom* and Gomorrah . . . are set forth for an example, suffering the vengeance of eternal fire.[1]

[1] Jude 6, 7.

The same comparison is made by Peter, who adds that Sodom was reduced to *ashes*.[1] In other words, the eternal fire mentioned in Jude is eternal in its *effect;* for no one will claim that the doomed city is now enveloped in flames. But if the fire reduced Sodom to *ashes*, and that destruction is *eternal*, then it can never be restored. Hence the very "example unto those that after should live ungodly" is one of unending ruin. It will be noticed in the above quotation that the overthrow of the wicked angels is "*even as* Sodom," and we are distinctly told by Christ that the lake of fire is "prepared for the devil and his angels," and John in vision saw the devil cast into that lake. Certainly, then, the devil and his angels cannot be restored, or else they apostatize again afterward; for ultimately they are destroyed in the second death. Thus from whichever side we study the doom of these wicked men and angels, there is no hope of their restoration. But if it could be shown that Sodom will be restored, it would be impossible to disprove the same for Satan and his companions.

Now we can advance a step, and notice another scripture where Sodom is compared with Israel: —

As I live, saith the Lord God, Sodom thy sister hath not done, she nor her daughters, as thou hast done, thou and thy daughters, . . . neither hath Samaria committed half of thy sins. . . . When I shall bring again their captivity, the captivity of Sodom and her daughters, and the captivity of Samaria and her daughters, then will I bring again the

[1] 2 Peter 2: 4-6.

captivity of thy captives in the midst of them. . . . When thy sisters, Sodom and her daughters, shall return to their former estate, and Samaria and her daughters shall return to their former estate, then thou and thy daughters shall return to your former estate. For thy sister Sodom was not mentioned by thy mouth in the day of thy pride.[1]

Strangely enough, this is the very passage which is supposed to teach most clearly the restoration of Sodom, because it is promised at the same time that Israel shall return. And in case Israel *is* to be restored, then it is certain that Sodom will be at the same time; and as before shown, then Satan will be released from his ruin. But notice more carefully; this scripture does not assert that Sodom and Samaria *will* be restored, but it is an indirect way of saying that Israel will *not* be restored. It is not a promise to Sodom and Samaria of a future redemption, but it is a keenly ironical way of stating that Israel has no hope. The Lord presents an impossible supposition to show Israel that her destruction is complete. She can no more be restored than Sodom — the very example of God's eternal vengeance. When Sodom can escape from her ashes, then — and not till then — can Israel return to her former estate. To illustrate, one might say, "When God shall abdicate his throne, truth will be only a lie." This does not assert that God *will* leave his throne. But it does indirectly but emphatically declare that truth can never be false; for God will always be God.

[1] Eze. 16 : 48-56.

This understanding of the passage is in perfect harmony with all other texts which speak of the destiny of Sodom, Israel, and Satan. It also corresponds with the withering sarcasm of the language to Israel in other parts of the chapter. It agrees with the direct assertion of Christ that in the day of judgment it will be more tolerable for Sodom than for the cities of Israel where he had taught. He did not imply that Sodom would be restored,— much less that Israel would be,— but that the relative guilt was in Sodom's favor. This is also consistent with the further words of the chapter quoted; for the Lord did confirm the new covenant — the everlasting covenant renewed — with the literal, national Israel, before she was left to her wanton ways to receive Sodom and Samaria as her companions in shame. Thus the heaviest batteries of this citadel of the future-age restoration theory are turned squarely against the return of any wicked nation after one entire probation of despising God's grace. Is not this in conformity with the perfect character of God? Why should he not put forth all his power to save men *now*, instead of destroying them once, and then restoring them to precisely the same condition for another trial? He himself asks what more he could do for his people Israel than has already been done. Divine love is *now* manifested to the fullest possible extent. Another probation could do no more in this respect, but it would increase the sin of men who had already rejected all the power of God in the gospel. Men who talk of a "better age" reveal the fact that they are ignorant of the grace of God for the present time.

REPENTANCE IMPOSSIBLE.

It is true that God will never reject any person who truly repents. If another probation would actually change the hearts of men, we might conclude that such a period would have been ordained. But it is a fact that truth ultimately refused places a man beyond the possibility of a genuine repentance. God has not changed; he has not arbitrarily decreed that after a certain season sinners will not be received; but the transgressor fixes his own doom by driving away the Spirit, until it becomes impossible to recognize his voice. This condition is described in Heb. 6 : 4–8. Evidently the unbelieving Jews had reached that point in their experience; for they attributed the miracles of Christ to the influence of Satan.[1] Hence the Holy Spirit could not convince them of sin. Christ showed them their fearful state as follows: —

> Whosoever speaketh a word against the Son of Man, it shall be forgiven him; but whosoever speaketh against the Holy Ghost, it shall not be forgiven him, *neither in this world, neither in the world to come.*[2]

Here we have a direct statement from the highest authority that the sin against the Holy Ghost

---

[1] Matt. 12 : 24.   [2] Matt. 12 : 32.

cannot be forgiven in the world to come. This does not imply that other sins will be pardoned in a future age; but it shows that only the sin which cannot be forgiven in this world, and which will be charged against the finally impenitent, will be recognized in the world to come. In other words, nothing but sin against the Holy Ghost can keep a person from forgiveness in this world; consequently all who do not now find forgiveness before their present probation closes, will bar forever the possibility of repentance, and therefore another life in the "world to come" would not change their course. This agrees exactly with the conclusions of a previous chapter that each one is responsible only for the light bestowed upon him; and that to disregard this light, whether less or more, will bring total darkness, and nothing can ever change his course. Hence in *love* and *mercy* — not in *anger* — God closes the destiny of mankind with this brief life.

Christ spoke in plain terms to the wicked people of Israel. They could never go where he was to go; for they *would die in their sins*. He considered death to be the end of their probation. But it may be objected that he was going to the Father; and while they can never go to heaven, they may be saved in a future age, and live on this earth. This inference, however, is disproved by his language to the same class, if not to the same persons, on another occasion: "Ye serpents, ye generation of vipers, how can ye escape the damnation of hell?"[1] He knew nothing of any degree of salvation for them. Only the damnation of hell awaited them.

But why say more? The whole teaching of the Bible is against a future restoration or salvation for any nation or person who neglects the present day of grace. Be not deceived by specious arguments or eloquent phrases about the love of God in a future age, for those who are lost in the present age. God will not change. He will not love the sinner either less or more than he does now. But the trouble is that the sinner does not love God now, and a future age would only increase his hate.

THE SORROW OF PAUL.

Notice the extreme anxiety of Paul as expressed in the words: —

> I say the truth in Christ, I lie not, my conscience also bearing me witness in the Holy Ghost, that I have great heaviness and continual sorrow in my heart. For I could wish that myself were accursed from Christ for my brethren, my kinsmen according to the flesh.[2]

Had Paul thought that a future restoration awaited all Israel, every one of his kinsmen, would he have been willing to lose his hope in Christ for them? But on the supposition, or the certainty rather, that they would be irrevocably lost if they did not then believe, his awful grief is reasonable;

---
[1] Matt. 23: 33.   [2] Rom. 9: 1-3.

so, too, when he labored publicly and from house to house night and day with tears, fearing for the loss of his converts, and even that he himself might be a castaway. Such anxiety and such labor are unknown to those who expect a better age. Let the gospel preached by Paul be preached again, and the church will awake, and the world will tremble. But a deathly stupor now holds people in the coils of the serpent. While men foolishly talk of Satan's redemption, he weaves the snare about their feet forever. While they look to a future age, the present one is slipping from their grasp.

These errors are easily discovered when the Lord's own definition of Israel is received. No future age is necessary to develop them; for they are the ones who, from the days of Adam and Abel to the end of the present age, receive the gospel in faith. All the unfulfilled promises to Irsael can be applied to them without going contrary to any portion of the revealed word. We do not deny a future regeneration of this earth, or that true Israel will live upon it forever, with Christ to reign personally over them on David's throne. All these points will be discussed in subsequent chapters. But we do say, with all the earnestness of a firm conviction, that there is no regeneration in a future age for any wicked person or nation. Instead of the conclusion of the Eastern Question marking the dawn of a new gospel age, it will end in the withdrawal of the only gospel ever committed to the human race. For manifest reasons, we cannot mention in detail each step in either direction; but principles are presented which will guide the reader in his further personal study of the great subject. We have touched a few of the texts considered the most conclusive on the side of a universal regeneration, and have found that they directly condemn the theory.

Chapter Six.

"ANOTHER GOSPEL."

"ANOTHER GOSPEL" is an expression once used in the Bible to denote false doctrines taught for the true gospel. There were men in the early days of the Christian era who were opposed to the truth set forth especially by the apostle Paul. His great theme was faith in Christ as the only avenue to the favor of God, and that this way was open to all men alike without distinction of birth or nation. His opponents held that the literal Israel were the chosen people; and that no salvation was possible without conformity to certain outward forms peculiar to the natural descendants of Abraham. The whole question turned on circumcision. Paul argued that true circumcision was a converted heart, and that to trust in some human mark in the flesh, was really to deny the power of God in the gospel. The others insisted that, notwithstanding all qualifications of character, "except ye be circumcised after the manner of Moses, ye cannot be saved."[1] This act, they taught, would connect the Gentiles with the Hebrew nation, and thus with the promises of God to

[1] Acts 15:1.

Israel. In their minds, the natural race distinction was an essential matter. They were quite willing that other nations should be blessed, provided it was done through their national prerogatives.

In contrast with their narrow ideas, Paul advocated the perfect equality of all men and nations, and urged that none of them could receive the promise of Abraham on a national basis. All alike must be grafted into Christ before they were Israelites. He claimed that his gospel was not of man, but by a direct revelation from Jesus Christ. In that revelation he saw the divine truth "that the Gentiles should be fellow heirs, and of the same body, and partakers of his promise in Christ by the gospel."[1] This had been the purpose of God from the beginning of the world, but through the blindness of men it had not been fully manifested. Not only had the apostle taught this vital feature of the gospel, but also that Jew and Gentile are equally invited at the same time and on the same conditions. He assures all alike that "*now* is the day of salvation." Not once does he intimate that a future age will come when those who neglect the present salvation will be granted another probation under more favorable circumstances. He does not expect that unbelieving Israel will be saved in some age to come. The whole life and teaching of Paul shows that he had no hope of a second probation for those who die in unbelief.

Suppose that the great apostle should now be

[1] Eph. 3 : 6.

able to hear men argue that all the Hebrew race are yet to be restored to Palestine, and be saved in an age subsequent to the appearing of the Lord; also that national distinctions are to be revived among the saved in that period, so that Israel as a nation will have the pre-eminence; and lastly that all the Gentiles and heathen will then occupy a subordinate position among the redeemed; would he not exclaim, "This is another gospel!" instead of recognizing it as the message which he once preached? What would be his feelings and words if he found this false theory extensively advocated by persons professing to teach the gospel of Christ? Though dead, he yet speaks, and this is what he says:—

> I marvel that ye are so soon removed from Him that called you into the grace of Christ unto *another gospel;* which is not another; but there be some that trouble you, and would pervert the gospel of Christ. But though we, or an angel from heaven, preach any other gospel unto you than that which we have preached unto you, let him be accursed. As we said before, so say I now again, *If any man preach any other gospel unto you than that ye have received, let him be accursed.*[1]

With all respect for honest though misguided men who teach a second probation in a future age, the return and salvation of the literal Jews, and various degrees of honor among the nations of the saved, we are constrained to say that in no respect does this theory conform to the gospel preached by

[1] Gal. 1:6-9.

Paul. It is emphatically "another gospel," a perverted gospel, which is not the true at all. As pointed out in a previous chapter, the restoration of Israel as a nation logically leads to the restoration of evil angels; and this view is now advocated openly by some who hold the former opinion. Is it not natural for Satan to desire a restoration to his former estate, or else try to show that God is not infinite love? If he can lead men to believe that Israel are to be restored to their former estate, then the next step is to teach that Sodom and all other wicked men are to be restored to their former estate, and finally they will endorse the whole thing, and include the devil and his evil companions in a universal salvation. Has God proclaimed such a message, or is it a theory invented by Satan,— "an angel from heaven," with "another gospel"?

GOD'S ELECT PEOPLE.

The theory of dispensational salvation by different gospels leads to the belief that there are several classes among the redeemed. Righteousness is based on a graded scale. Various bodies of "elect" are formed to correspond with each age. It is a kind of religious caste; a divine aristocracy; a sort of gospel Freemasonry with appropriate degrees of honor. In one age the saved are supposed to reach the highest pinnacle of glory; in another period the saved get about half way up to the top; and in still another dispensation, the restored can never get above the lowest plane at the base. Thus the *time* when a person happens to be born fixes his position in the "society" of heaven. Thus it is taught that now — in the present dispensation — God is gathering out an elect body, the church, to be the "bride" of Christ; that in the former dispensation he was engaged in saving an elect nation — Israel; and that in a future age he will complete the work for Israel, which has been interrupted for the past eighteen hundred years by the calling out of the "bride." In other words, it is held that the present age is parenthetical — a period interjected into the purpose of God to save Israel. He began with the Hebrew nation, but after a two thousand years' effort broke them off temporarily while he took up the more pressing work of saving the bride; and when she is brought out, he will again take up the case of Israel, and save them. Thus, while Abraham, Isaac, and Jacob will be saved as part of Israel, the "elect nation," they cannot associate with Christians in this age, the church, which will constitute the "elect bride." Highest in honor will of course be the "bride," next will come Israel, the "elect nation." Lower still will be the great multitude saved in the future millennial age under the influence of the bride and Israel; and perhaps lowest of all will be Satan and his host.

Some make still other sub-divisions; with them the "bride" is only a select few out of the present age, who will be "caught up" secretly to meet the Lord in the air; then the "church," composed of ordinary Christians, will be saved at the visible appearing of Christ; after that, the Jews, or Israel, — the "elect nation," — will be gathered; and finally all nations will be gathered in another great multitude.

The mere mention of such a medley should be a sufficient refutation of the entire system logically connected with it. God is not the author of confusion. The gospel is exceedingly simple; but its true nature is almost obscured by human inventions. But if the evil principle of special salvations in different ages is admitted, there is no limit to the number of gospels which may be proposed to develop the various "elect" bodies. It is bad enough to have men in this life divided into classes by caste, color, wealth, birth, education, etc.; but what shall be said if such lines are to be eternally drawn among the redeemed?

In contrast with this Babel of error, notice the divine truth that God has only one "elect" in all the universe, and that is JESUS CHRIST: —

Behold my servant, whom I uphold; *mine elect*, in whom my soul delighteth; I have put my Spirit upon him: he shall bring forth judgment to the Gentiles.[1] Behold I lay in Zion a chief corner-stone, *elect*, precious; and he that believeth on him shall not be confounded.[2]

Christ, the "Elect," is set forth to all the world. He is the same "yesterday, to-day, and forever,"

[1] Isa. 42 : 1. [2] 1 Peter 2 : 6.

and the invitation is extended to all; "whosoever will may come." Every one who responds is thereby numbered with the "elect."

> And ye are complete in Him, which is the head of all principality and power.[1] According as he hath chosen us in him; . . . wherein he hath made us accepted in the Beloved.[2]

There is no election for any individual until he receives Christ. Hence we are admonished to "make our calling and election sure." It is a thing which depends on our acceptance of the gospel in Christ. He who has the "Elect" is elected.

Christ is not divided; therefore he who has Christ at all, has all the fulness of God. There can be no grades of salvation or of righteousness. It is all of Christ, or it is nothing. Hence there can be no grades among the elect in Christ. He is the same to all men in all ages. What he was to Wesley or Luther, he was to Abraham or Abel. What he was to these, he was, and is, and will be, to every individual who is ever saved. The degree of light seen by men may differ, but the light is the same to all. Faithfulness with one talent or five talents will bring the same reward.

Thus we are brought to the conclusion that there is only one elect body for all ages and for all people. That body is called by different names, but it is the same people. It is the "church," or it is true Israel. The "church" embraces all the

[1] Col. 2 : 10. [2] Eph. 1 : 4-6.

redeemed of all ages; "Israel" includes precisely the same. Christians belong to both. All who are Christ's are Christians; all who are Christ's are Abraham's seed, or Israelites; all who are Christ's belong to his body, the church; all who are Christ's are the elect. Consequently there is not a particle of difference among those who are called "Israel," "Christians," "the church," and "the elect." One Saviour is for all the race; one gospel is the message for all; and one body of believers is the result. This grand doctrine is everywhere set forth in the Scriptures, and we will quote a few texts: —

And other sheep I have, which are not of this fold; them also I must bring, and they shall hear my voice; *and there shall be one fold*, and one shepherd.[1] That in the dispensation of the fulness of times he might gather together in *one* all things in Christ, both which are in heaven, and which are on earth; even in him.[2] There is one body, and one Spirit, even as ye are called in one hope of your calling; one Lord, one faith, one baptism, one God and Father of all, who is above all, and through all, and in you all.[3]

It would be as reasonable to teach that God, the Lord, and the Holy Spirit are each several beings, as it is to say that there are several elect companies, each with a different hope, a different faith, and a different body.

Paul especially emphasizes the fact that by means of Christ both Jews and Gentiles are made one household. In Eph. 2 : 12 he reminds the Gen-

[1] John 10 : 16. [2] Eph. 1 : 10. [3] Eph. 4 : 3-6.

tiles that they had no hope, no God, no Christ, no part in the covenants of promise, while they were aliens from the commonwealth of Israel. They must receive the same gospel that was committed to Abraham and to the Hebrews. All could be made nigh by the blood of Christ: —

> For through him we both have access by one Spirit unto the Father. Now therefore ye are no more strangers and foreigners, but fellow citizens with the saints, and of the household of God; and are built upon the foundation of the apostles and prophets, Jesus Christ himself being the chief corner-stone.[1]

In short, all the perplexing distinctions invented by men to separate Israel from Gentiles, the church and the bride from ordinary Christians, are swept aside by the word of God. Christ could express no higher reward than to say, "Many shall come from the east and west, and shall sit down with Abraham, and Isaac, and Jacob, in the kingdom of heaven."[2] We remember that the Jews who were so intent on proving that they were the "elect," missed any place in the kingdom. The chosen disciples were so busy discussing the relative honor that each should receive that they did not comprehend the teaching of Christ. We greatly fear that in these days the same result will befall men who are wasting time on hair-splitting questions respecting the superiority of Jews over Gentiles, or of the members of the bride over Christians generally. Having mistaken God's defi-

[1] Eph. 2 : 18-20. [2] Matt. 8 : 11.

nition of Israel, they will not recognize the chosen ones any more than the Jews did Christ, and like them they will spare a robber and murderer, while condemning the elect of God to shameful suffering. It will be well for all to take a low seat until the Master shall say, "Come up higher." The first shall be last, and the last first. The very spirit which prompts men to assign the best positions to themselves is evidence that they are not worthy to receive them.

MUTILATING SCRIPTURE.

To maintain these various ideas of separate dispensations, for different-grade gospels to save diverse elect bodies, the Scriptures are treated with great dishonor, and yet with much asserted regard for their contents. Nothing they say is directly denied; but they are so analyzed and explained that the most extravagant vagaries pass for solemn truth. The most minute care must be exercised so that a blessing promised to the "bride" shall not be applied to men of God like Abraham or Daniel who lived in a former dispensation. Equal concern is manifested in teaching Gentiles that they must avoid anything spoken to Israel—even the ten commandments. Sect after sect comes up, each with a new theory, until the head is dizzy, trying to reach the top of Babylon's tower. Under the impression that they are rightly dividing the word of God, the book is made a jargon of conflicting creeds as foolish as the questions discussed by the Pharisees of old; and those who are confused in the endless discussions of warring factions, are fast losing true reverence for the Bible.

JUDGED BY THEIR FRUIT.

We have pointed out something of the terrible conditions existing among the professed followers of Christ. All Christian bodies deplore it, but what is the remedy? We boldly assert that the prevalent false ideas about Israel are responsible for much of the confusion. On that rock the ancient Hebrew nation struck. Disregarding God's description of true circumcision in the heart, they trusted in the fleshly mark made by human hands. Forgetting the blessing that made Jacob Israel, they thought birth, nationality, was everything. So, again, men say little about the character of the true Israel, but they are full of ideas about the national Israel. In accordance with this, the dealings of God with his people in the past age are entirely separated from his dealings with them in the present age, while probation in a future age is looked for to complete their plan. Of course this creates different classes among the redeemed, and then different portions of the Bible must be made to "fit." Then a host of churches, chapels, missions, halls, streets, parks, etc., must be used to teach each theory. The total result is a mass of error, a terrible din, and the loss of souls.

It is no wonder that the world turns away from the exhibition with scorn; no wonder that the exhausted factions sigh for the millennium, when it is thought that rest and peace will come. But if men would only rest a moment *now*, and learn what Israel really means, they would see that much of their zeal is useless and positively dangerous. They would learn that *this* is the age when God's love abounds equally to all men.

In both doctrine and fruits the prevalent ideas concerning Israel are proved false. And while these errors engross the minds of men, and they anticipate the speedy fulfilment of their dreams, the Eastern Question is waiting for the fulness of the Gentiles to come in, the remnant of Israel to be gathered out of all nations, and then the calamities involved in this question will break in wrath upon an unprepared world and a deluded church. "Another gospel" is taught, and as a result strange children are begotten.

Chapter Seven.

THE PROMISED LAND.

BY a sixfold investigation on entirely separate and independent lines, we have found only one conclusion possible, namely, that the inheritance is promised to the true Israel, comprising all who are really Christ's followers; and no further argument on this subject is necessary. Now we turn our attention to the location where they will dwell. Will Jerusalem be their place of abode? Will Palestine come under their control? This opens up an interesting phase of the Eastern Question; for Turkey now controls the ancient Holy Land. Is this effete government to be dispossessed of its territory in Asia as well as in Europe? Many have expected that the Jews would yet return to their former home and establish a kingdom under the reign of Christ on David's throne; but we have found that this is impossible. Will true Israel fulfil this expectation, or is this theory also incorrect? Where is the promised land? Is it on this earth or in heaven? or is it in both places or in neither of them? Go with us as we run the surveyor's chain which is to measure three worlds before the bounds of Israel's territory are meted out.

THE OLD WORLD.

First in order the Bible speaks of "*the old world.*" To locate the time and place of its existence we read concerning its brief history and destiny that God "spared not *the old world*, but saved Noah the eighth person, a preacher of righteousness, bringing in the flood upon the world of the ungodly."[1]

Here we learn that this earth from creation to the flood constituted *the old world*. Let us go back to the "beginning," and learn more about its original condition and purpose. "Very good"[2] was the verdict of the great Creator, as he surveyed the new world which had emerged from the primitive chaos; and we are also told that when the foundations thereof were laid, "the morning stars sang together, and all the sons of God shouted for joy."[3] The happy occupant of this world was man, made in the image of God. For his use the garden of Eden was prepared as the first home on earth; and as his posterity increased, the whole world would have been filled with similar dwellings of love and beauty. In the most explicit manner Adam and his descendants were given dominion over the earth and all upon it. There can be no question that this earth was the place originally prepared for the home of a righteous race of men

[1] 2 Peter 2: 5. [2] Gen. 1: 31. [3] Job 38: 7.

— not one country alone, of limited extent, but all the world.

The dominion thus bestowed on man was lost when he turned away from the word of God to believe the serpent's lie. In consequence of Adam's sin, the race was doomed to death, and the ground was destined to bring forth thorns and thistles. The hope of a coming Deliverer was set before the sinful race — another Man, the second Adam, who should redeem what had been lost. This plan of redemption must embrace the earth, as well as man, and it is a remarkable fact that Christ did bear the very curse of the ground, in a *crown of thorns* placed in mockery on his brow. Hence the Bible speaks of the "redemption of the purchased possession" when the gospel is finished. But that old world perished in the flood without the fulfilment of the divine plan, and therefore we next observe —

THE PRESENT WORLD.

In distinction from the old world, which perished, the Scriptures speak of "this present evil world," or "the heavens and the earth which are now." Of course the different worlds refer to the same material planet, this earth, but changed in appearance and structure. Many beautiful things are still seen, notwithstanding the heavy curse that rests on the face of nature; but how great the contrast must now be to the original home of man in the newly created paradise. This may indeed be called the "present *evil* world;" for dark has been its record of sin and crime under the dominion of Satan. But even in its present condition, groaning under the curse while it waits for redemption, it is not forgotten by Him who notices the sparrow's fall, and who is gathering out of the sin-swept world an Israel for his glory. To Noah, the second great father of the race, immediately after the flood, the covenant of grace to the earth and its inhabitants was renewed: —

While the earth remaineth, seed-time and harvest, and cold and heat, and summer and winter, and day and night shall not cease.[1] And I, behold, I establish my covenant with you, and with your seed after you; and with every living creature that is with you, of the fowl, of the cattle, and of every beast of the earth with you; from all that go out of the ark, to every beast of the earth. And I will establish my covenant with you; neither shall all flesh be cut off any more by the waters of a flood; neither shall there any more be a flood to destroy the earth. And God said, This is the token of the covenant which I make between me and you and every living creature that is with you, for perpetual generations; I do set my bow in the cloud, and it shall be for a token of a covenant between me and the earth. And it shall come to pass, when I bring a cloud over the earth, that the bow shall be seen in the cloud. . . . And I will look upon it, that I may remember the everlasting covenant between God and every living creature of all flesh that is upon the earth.[2]

What a wonderful interest does our God manifest in the earth that it should be the subject of

[1] Gen. 8: 22. [2] Gen. 9: 9-16.

such a gracious covenant; and what a beautiful "token" has he given in the rainbow arch, encircling the world in the time of storm, even as the same "bow of promise" is ever seen above his eternal throne.

But this sin-scarred earth is not always to continue in its present condition. God's covenant embraces a fairer world than this for the final inheritance of his people. Another world, the third and last, called —

"THE WORLD TO COME,"

Is yet to rise upon the horizon of God's eternal purpose. Another flood — not of water, but of fire — will engulf this sin-stricken planet, and upon its purified foundations will stand a new world, to the eternal praise of God's grace, and for the everlasting happiness of his people. Peter describes these three worlds in the order of their succession, as follows: —

Whereby the world that then was, being overflowed with water, perished; but the heavens and the earth which are now, by the same word are kept in store, reserved unto fire against the day of judgment and perdition of ungodly men. . . . Nevertheless we, according to his promise, look for *new heavens and a new earth*, wherein dwelleth righteousness.[1]

Now, in which of these worlds will the true Israel of God receive their inheritance? Will it be in any part of this "evil world," or will it be in the

[1] 2 Peter 3: 6, 7, 13.

purified "world to come"? Are they to be gathered to Palestine, now so barren and under the rule of an apostate power, or will their "promised land" be upon the new earth? The answer is already on our lips; but before it is uttered let us notice —

THE LAND PROMISED TO ABRAHAM.

Now the Lord had said unto Abram, Get thee out of thy country, and from thy kindred, and from thy father's house, unto a land that I will show thee.[1]

This promise is afterward repeated with more emphatic detail: —

And the Lord said unto Abram, after that Lot was separated from him, Lift up now thine eyes, and look from the place where thou art, northward, and southward, and eastward, and westward; for all the land which thou seest, to thee will I give it, and to thy seed forever. . . . Arise, walk through the land in the length of it and in the breadth of it; for I will give it unto thee.[2]

Thrice afterward is the promise repeated, and finally confirmed by the oath of God, that by two immutable things — the promise and the oath — the heirs of promise "might have a strong consolation, who have fled for refuge, to lay hold on the hope set before us."[3] Nothing can exceed the certainty of this inheritance. God cannot lie.

Let it be observed that the land promised to Abraham was not confined to a limited territory; for Paul writes of it as follows: —

[1] Gen. 12:1.   [2] Gen. 13:14-17.   [3] Heb. 6:13-20.

For the promise, that he should be the *heir of the world*, was not to Abraham, or to his seed, through the law, but through the righteousness of faith.[1]

Now a very important question arises as to *which world* was promised to Abraham and his seed. Is it "this present evil world," or is it "the world to come"? A definite answer is found in the words of Stephen: —

> And he said, Men, brethren, and fathers, hearken. The God of glory appeared unto our father Abraham, when he was in Mesopotamia, before he dwelt in Charran, and said unto him, Get thee out of thy country, and from thy kindred, and come into the land which I shall show thee. Then came he out of the land of the Chaldeans, and dwelt in Charran; and from thence, when his father was dead, he removed him into this land, wherein ye now dwell. *And he gave him none inheritance in it, no, not so much as to set his foot on;* yet he promised that he would give it to him for a possession, etc.[2]

When Stephen spoke these words, Abraham had long been dead. He lived on *this world* one hundred and seventy-five years, and about half of the whole period in the land of *Canaan;* but *he never even once set his foot on the promised inheritance.* Here is unmistakable evidence that neither this whole world nor the land of Canaan constitutes the territory God promised to Abraham and his seed. It must therefore be found in "the world to come," or else the oath-bound word of Jehovah will fail. The latter is not possible, and the only

[1] Rom. 4:13.   [2] Acts 7:2-5.

conclusion is, that the "promised land" is the *new earth yet to be created.*

A HEAVENLY COUNTRY.

Abraham, and his righteous seed, the real Israel, understood the true nature of the inheritance. They never expected that the promise would be fulfilled in the present world; this is shown by the language of Paul: —

These all died in faith, not having received the promises, but having seen them afar off, and were persuaded of them, and embraced them, and confessed that they were *strangers and pilgrims on the earth.* For they that say such things declare plainly that they *seek a country.* And truly, if they had been mindful of that country from whence they came out, they might have had opportunity to have returned. But now they desire a *better country*, that is, *an heavenly;* wherefore God is not ashamed to be called their God; for he hath prepared for them a city.[1]

THE NEW JERUSALEM.

Numerous promises to Israel pertain to a city called Jerusalem, and those who look only for the national restoration of the Jews to Palestine expect that old Jerusalem will again be built up and beautified. This is not the teaching of the Bible, however. Abraham looked for a city which God shall build, and the description of such a place occupies the closing chapters of the Holy Book. New Jerusalem is its name. Now it is located "above;" but finally it comes down to be the capital of Israel's kingdom on the new earth. For beauty,

---

[1] Heb. 11 : 13-16.

the city is compared to a bride adorned for her husband; her raiment is the righteousness of saints; her food is the fruit of the tree of life, and her drink the water of the river of life. Here, at last, will Israel be gathered. Here the promises will be fulfilled.

O, is it not a pity that so many professing Christians now have no higher hope for Abraham's seed than some part of this old earth, when the Lord has promised something so much "better," even a "*heavenly*" country? How can he help being "ashamed" of those who do not believe his word on this point, and so waste their time, strength, and means, teaching any to look to the barren land of Judea as the place of rest? No promises of any kind are for the national Israel after the flesh, and no place on this present world will ever be the home of God's children. The land of Palestine will never echo with the tread of a redeemed nation, and old Jerusalem will never be the dwelling-place of those whom Christ shall gather from every land. A better country is theirs. Their "land" is the "world to come," and their city the New Jerusalem. They have no interest in the strife of nations over the possession of the land of Judea, except as it may indicate the near approach of the "world to come," where their hearts and treasures are placed. The Eastern Question may obscure the political heavens; but they still see the "bow of promise" in the cloud.

Beyond the storm of this world, they see the land of peace in "the world to come."

PARADISE RESTORED.

What pen can write, what tongue can tell, what mind can comprehend, the bliss of Israel in the world restored? Prophets from the beginning of the world have spoken of the "restitution of all things;"[1] but their thrilling words of inspiration must fall far below the actual reality. To Adam it will restore the long-lost Eden;[2] to Abraham it will bring the "heavenly country;"[3] to Moses it will bring the great recompense of the reward;[4] to true Israel it will be the promised land;[5] to David it will be the new earth, where the meek shall dwell;[6] to Isaiah it will be Beulah land;[7] to Daniel it will be the kingdom given to the saints of the Most High;[8] to Paul it will usher in the eternal weight of glory;[9] to Peter it will be the incorruptible inheritance;[10] to John it will be the new heavens and the new earth seen in vision;[11] to Christ it will bring an answer to the prayer, "Thy kingdom come. Thy will be done in earth, as it is in heaven;"[12] and to the Father it will be the accomplishment of his eternal purpose of love throughout all ages.[13]

[1] Acts 3:21. [2] Gen. 3:23, 24; Isa. 51:8.
[3] Heb. 11:8-10, 16. [4] Heb. 11:26. [5] Deut. 27:3; James 2:5.
[6] Ps. 37:11, 22, 29. [7] Isa. 62:4. [8] Dan. 7:27.
[9] 2 Cor. 4:17. [10] 1 Peter 1:4. [11] Rev. 21:1.
[12] Matt. 6:10. [13] 2 Tim. 1:9.

Earth and heaven will then be united; the tabernacle of God will be with men; the throne of God and the Lamb will be among them, and God himself will be with them and be their God, and they shall see his face.

And there shall be no more curse.[1] And God shall wipe away all tears from their eyes; and there shall be no more death, neither sorrow, nor crying, neither shall there be any more pain; for the former things are passed away.[2] Then the eyes of the blind shall be opened, and the ears of the deaf unstopped. Then shall the lame man leap as an hart, and the tongue of the dumb sing.[3] For ye shall go out with joy, and be led forth with peace; the mountains and the hills shall break forth before you into singing, and all the trees of the field shall clap their hands. Instead of the thorn shall come up the fir-tree, and instead of the brier shall come up the myrtle-tree.[4] The wilderness and the solitary place shall be glad for them; and the desert shall rejoice, and blossom as the rose.[5] The wolf also shall dwell with the lamb, and the leopard shall lie down with the kid; and the calf and the young lion and the fatling together; and a little child shall lead them. And the cow and the bear shall feed; their young ones shall lie down together; and the lion shall eat straw like the ox. . . . They shall not hurt nor destroy in all my holy mountain; for the earth shall be full of the knowledge of the Lord, as the waters cover the sea.[6]

GENERAL REMARKS.

The thoughtful reader will not fail to note the perfect harmony in this subject with what has gone before. Our temple of truth has many pillars, cut

[1] Rev. 22 : 3. [2] Rev. 21 : 4. [3] Isa. 35 : 5, 6.
[4] Isa. 55 : 12, 13. [5] Isa. 35 : 1. [6] Isa. 11 : 6–9.

from various quarries by different workmen; and yet when they are brought together in the erection of God's building, no sound of ax or hammer is heard. The builder and maker is God, and each part is exactly adjusted to its place. Not so is the structure built on plausible human theories. However beautiful and substantial it may appear, no Samson is needed to overthrow its flimsy foundations, and effect a ruin as great as that which befell the temple of Dagon at Gaza.

It is a deceitful voice that offers the hope of the world's conversion in a future age. Like a modern Delilah, it lulls men to sleep only that they may be shorn of their God-given strength. Is it not plain that there is truth in the arguments here presented? Have we not searched from Genesis to Revelation, comparing independent Scriptural lines? and in each line is there not unity in all its parts, while it is in perfect accord with the others, and with the whole Bible? Are these cunningly devised fables? Is the Bible given only to confuse and mislead? — No; every argument thus far adduced, like a strong link, has strengthened the chain of truth, and this will be found to be true of every argument yet to be presented.

We want the truth. When the gathering storm shall break in the settlement of the Eastern Question, we want to be built on the Rock.

Chapter Eight.

THE SANCTUARY.

IN our argument concerning Israel, the sanctuary is an essential feature. All who are acquainted with the history of the Hebrew nation, will at once recall the prominent place occupied by the sanctuary. It was the very center of the Hebrew religion, the chief object of interest in all their national life. In many respects they were a typical people, an ensample and warning to later generations. If the purpose of God concerning that nation is to be fulfilled by the true Israel, they must of necessity be closely connected with the sanctuary of Christ's ministry. Here, then, is abundant reason for introducing it in this discussion. Another reason for considering this subject is that it is made prominent in an important prophecy relative to time given in Dan. 8:14. Hence no one who feels an interest in the Scriptures, especially in the prophecies, can ignore this matter.

Then, again, this subject is by some supposed to teach that the land of Palestine is to be cleansed from the rule of the Turk and the false religion of Mohammed, in order that the Jews may return and be established as a kingdom under the reign of

Christ on David's throne. By previous argument it has been demonstrated that the Jews will never return as a nation, and it has also been shown that true Israel receive their inheritance in the world to come, and not in Palestine or Jerusalem. Consequently so much of the theory mentioned is already disproved, and the rest might be dismissed as unsound without further investigation. But we will not pass by the matter on these grounds. By applying the same sound principles which have thus far guided our study, we can examine this theory on its merits. If it leads to results in opposition to former conclusions, it will be necessary to revise our deductions accordingly, or else seek for further light, in order to make harmony. On the contrary, if this subject, when independently treated, agrees with previous conclusions, the correctness of the whole argument will be confirmed by fresh evidence.

Seven times already our paths have converged to the same general result. Will the eighth lead in an opposite direction? To this perfectly fair test we cheerfully submit. What, then, is the sanctuary? what is its cleansing? When will the cleansing take place?

WHAT IS THE SANCTUARY?

The word "sanctuary" means a sacred place. This idea is embodied in the original command of the Lord to the children of Israel, through Moses: "And let them make me a sanctuary; that I may dwell among them.'"[1] Then follow minute instructions relative to the wonderful structure which was to be honored with God's special presence. It contained two apartments, called the "holy" and the "most holy," separated by a veil of fine linen. In the first apartment, or holy place, were the golden candlestick, the table of showbread, and the altar of incense. The chief object of interest in the second apartment, or most holy place, was the ark of the testimony, with its top called the mercy-seat.

This movable tabernacle was in later times replaced by the permanent temple built by Solomon, and rebuilt by Zerubbabel and by Herod.

There can be no doubt that these various buildings constituted the sanctuary on earth for the Lord during nearly fifteen hundred years. Paul describes these apartments, and directly assures us that this building was the worldly sanctuary of the first covenant. These are his words: —

Then verily the first covenant had also ordinances of divine service, and a worldly sanctuary. For there was a tabernacle made; the first, wherein was the candlestick, and the table, and the showbread; which is called the sanctuary. And after the second veil, the tabernacle which is called the holiest of all; which had the golden censer, and the ark of the covenant overlaid round about with gold, wherein was the golden pot that had manna, and Aaron's rod that budded, and the tables of the covenant; and over it the cherubim of glory shadowing the mercy-seat; of which we cannot now speak particularly.[2]

[1] Ex. 25:8. [2] Heb. 9:1-5.

THE SANCTUARY.

Probably no one will deny that the "first covenant," which is here mentioned, continued until Christ died on the cross — until the moment that he said, "It is finished;" "and, behold, the veil of the temple was rent in twain from the top to the bottom."[1] Thus God signified the exact moment when that temple service could no more be acceptable. During the fifteen hundred years covered by Paul's testimony, we know precisely what constituted the sanctuary. Notice: it was not Palestine as a country; nor Jerusalem as a city; nor Mount Zion, on which the temple stood; but it was a *building*, first erected by Moses, and replaced by the temples of Solomon, Zerubbabel, and Herod. Certainly the sanctuary of that period was not the land, nor the city, nor the people. It was a special habitation for the Lord's service. There is no reason at all for men to apply the word to anything else except just what the Bible states the sanctuary to be, namely, a building made with hands of men.

THE SANCTUARY A PATTERN.

But it may be asked if the sanctuary does not symbolize the land of Palestine or Jerusalem? The answer is, *No*, for two reasons; first, the Bible does not so use the word; and, secondly, we are distinctly told that it represents an entirely different thing. That the sanctuary built by Moses was only a "pattern," we are assured in the directions given by the Lord. Paul also calls it a "figure," and its service

[1] Matt. 27:51.

an "example," a "shadow," etc. Was it a "pattern" of the land of Palestine? Was it a figure of Jerusalem? The absurdity of such applications must be apparent. Now let Paul tell what it did represent : —

Now of the things which we have spoken this is the sum: We have such an high priest, who is set on the right hand of the throne of the Majesty in the heavens; a minister of the *sanctuary, and of the true tabernacle, which the Lord pitched, and not man.*[1]

The sanctuary built by man is a type of the true sanctuary, which the Lord has pitched. Who ministers in the true sanctuary? — Jesus, our High Priest. Where does he minister? — At "the right hand of the throne of the Majesty in the heavens." Then where is the true sanctuary? — In heaven, where Christ ministers as priest. But does he not minister on earth too? — "*For if he were on earth*, HE SHOULD NOT BE A PRIEST."[2] Christ's work as priest is all done in heaven. He never will minister on earth in that capacity. He will never do any priestly service at Jerusalem. Why will he not be a priest in Palestine or anywhere else on earth? For three reasons: 1. The work on earth ended with the old covenant. 2. It would be contrary to the "law" for any one except a Levite to act as priest on earth; and "it is evident that our Lord sprang out of Judah; of which tribe Moses spake nothing concerning priesthood."[3] 3. Because there is no sanctuary on earth in which

---
[1] Heb. 8: 1, 2.   [2] Heb. 8: 4.   [3] Heb. 7: 14.

the work could be done. Even if it could be shown that Jerusalem is the sanctuary to be cleansed, Christ could not minister there according to the "law."

Thus by overwhelming evidence are we obliged to recognize the fact that there is no sanctuary on this earth, but there is one in heaven; and in that true sanctuary, "which the Lord pitched," the work of Christ as priest will be done "once for all." There is no confusion here; thus far each step is made sure by plain words of Scripture.

We repeat: the sanctuary of the first covenant was one definite thing — a building minutely described, and used for a certain purpose. That was a pattern of the true sanctuary in heaven, where Christ began his work as priest when he had first offered himself as a sacrifice on the cross as the Lamb of God. Neither of these sanctuaries represents Palestine or Jerusalem. All the service on earth was to be done by Levites, but Christ is of the tribe of Judah. Hence if he were on earth, he should not be a priest. "Christ is not entered into the holy places made with hands, which are the figures of the true; but into heaven itself, now to appear in the presence of God for us."[1] If these statements are given due weight, it will be seen that they entirely disprove the idea that Christ is ever to be a priest on this earth.

There is further proof that the sanctuary is in heaven. John in vision saw the temple of God

[1] Heb. 9:24.

opened in heaven, and therein he saw the ark of his testament.[1] He also saw the altar of incense and the seven lamps of fire before the throne.[2] The true sanctuary is "*in*" heaven; therefore it is not heaven itself. The earthly tabernacle was not a type of all heaven; but it was a "pattern of things *in* the heavens." John, in viewing the sanctuary as above mentioned, did not see heaven open, but he did see a *temple in heaven* open; and that temple has a "door," for John saw a "*door*" opened in heaven. In short, the true sanctuary is a building, or temple, in which the throne of God is placed, and where the work of Christ is performed. This temple, like the "pattern," must have two apartments, or holy places, in each of which Christ is to minister. The claim that his ministry is only in one place, and without change from beginning to end, is contrary to plainly stated facts. The pattern had two places, and so has the true sanctuary.

Note also the fact that when John saw the "door" opened in heaven, he describes the articles of furniture used in the first apartment, and later, when again the "temple was opened," he saw the ark, which was always kept in the second apartment. Had there been but one room, he would have seen all the things mentioned without another door opening later.

There is no reasonable objection to the idea of

[1] Rev. 11:19.   [2] Rev. 8:3; 4:5.

a literal building in heaven. The Bible speaks of a "temple;" it has a "door;" and it is in the "city" whose "builder and maker is God." The sanctuary is a real place, a definite habitation for the great "I AM." No one claims that it is made of the crude materials used in this world.

A more plausible objection may arise from what is said in Dan. 8 : 13 about the sanctuary's being "trodden under foot." How can it be trodden under foot if it is in heaven?— In the same way that Christ is "trodden under foot," as stated in Heb. 10 : 29. When the provisions of God's grace are neglected, men are said to have "trodden under foot the Son of God," though he is in heaven. So the sanctuary has been "trodden under foot" by the indifference shown to its important place in the divine plan. For many centuries it has been obscured through incorrect ideas of the atonement; and those who would even now make it a part of Palestine or Jerusalem are treating it as a common thing of earth. But the time has come when the real significance of the sanctuary is understood by the true Israel, who will receive the benefit of the work now going on in its hallowed apartments. Perhaps one of the best tests of a true Israelite is the way he treats the subject of the sanctuary in heaven, and especially the cleansing in the most holy place. True Israel will recognize its use, and act accordingly. See Lev. 26 : 2.

THE CLEANSING.

What is the cleansing of the sanctuary? Having found that the "worldly sanctuary" is a pattern of the one in heaven, and that the priests on earth served unto the example and shadow of heavenly things, it will be easy to learn what the cleansing of the heavenly sanctuary is by studying as an object-lesson the work done in the earthly sanctuary for fifteen hundred years. Certainly the dullest pupil should learn a lesson repeated fifteen hundred times before his eyes.

Once every year the earthly sanctuary was cleansed. This was on the tenth day of the seventh month, also called the day of atonement. On this occasion the high priest alone went into the second apartment, the most holy place, and made an offering for all Israel. Any soul which did not take part in that solemn service was cut off from the congregation. No one could receive the benefit of the atonement without this service. Lots were cast between two goats, and the one selected for the Lord was killed, and with its blood the atonement was made. All the sins of the people were then put upon the head of the live goat, the scapegoat, and he was sent into the wilderness, bearing the load of guilt. This completed the round of service. Year by year this was performed for fifteen centuries. What did it shadow forth in the ministry of Christ, of which it was a type?

According to the "pattern," the work of Christ must be comprised in two divisions, one performed in the holy place, and another in the most holy. The first began immediately after the ascension, more than eighteen hundred years ago. In that first apartment the general work of the priestly office is performed, in the pardon of penitent believers by virtue of the blood shed on Calvary. This is a reality, not an imaginary service, a mere sentiment. Sin is a real thing; Christ is a real priest; the sanctuary is a real place; pardon is an actual fact. In the earthly service we see only the shadow; but in the true sanctuary we see the substance.

As each round of service in the worldly sanctuary closed with a special work of atonement called the cleansing of the sanctuary, so the true work in the heavenly sanctuary will close with a corresponding ministration. For this purpose the second apartment of the sanctuary is opened, and the work transferred thereto. There, before the Father and the angels, Christ will confess the names of his children, who have confessed him in this world. This is the final atonement for them; and their sins, canceled from the records of heaven, are then removed forever. In the earthly pattern the sins of Israel were placed on the scapegoat by the priest; so in the true work in heaven Christ will place the sins of true Israel on some other being. He no longer bears them himself, but they are transferred to the shoulders of the great scapegoat, *Satan*, the author of sin, in whose person every transgression, removed from the righteous, will meet its just recompense of reward. As the ancient scapegoat, laden with the sins of Israel, was banished from the camp and left to perish in the uninhabited wilderness, so Satan will be forever banished from the true Israel of God — no longer permitted access to them — when Christ shall have cleansed the heavenly sanctuary. This is the time when Satan is bound in the bottomless pit, an event which will be discussed more fully in following pages.

Can any one fail to see the tremendous importance of the subject before us, that the cleansing of the sanctuary is the finishing act in the service of our Priest? In the earthly sanctuary this service was performed every year — over and over for fifteen centuries — on purpose to teach men the nature of Christ's work in heaven. But with him there is only one round of service. His work is "once for all," and the cleansing of the true sanctuary will close his work as priest forever, and with it human probation. True Israel will then be made up and saved; the "fulness of the Gentiles" will have come in, and the eternal destiny of men will be decided.

By unmistakable logic from plain facts presented in the Scriptures, we are led to this conclusion. The solemn truths connected with this subject have not been duly understood or appreciated. The sanctuary has been "trodden under foot" by degrading it to some earthly position, by disregarding its true relation to the work of Christ in heaven, and by neglecting its gracious provisions. To the ancient Israelites the worldly sanctuary was the central object of interest. To true Israelites the heavenly sanctuary is the place of absorbing attention. Especially will this appear when we come to its cleansing. Is it near?

THE TWENTY-THREE HUNDRED DAYS.

The remaining question to be answered on this subject is, When will the sanctuary in heaven be cleansed? Daniel heard two holy beings in conversation on this matter, and the answer, addressed to the prophet, was, "Unto two thousand and three hundred days, then shall the sanctuary be cleansed." Here is a long prophetic period, and at its close the cleansing of the sanctuary is to occur. When does it end? We are not directly informed on this point; but we are told when it began, and, reckoning from that point, it is easy to find the close. Fortunately we are not left to human conjecture for an understanding of the prophecy; for while Daniel "sought for the meaning," the command was heard, "Gabriel, make this man to understand the vision."

We will not here follow all that the angel said in the remainder of the chapter concerning parts of the vision which precede the statement relative to the 2300 days. It is sufficient to notice that this period of time was not then explained, probably owing to the prophet's agitation and illness, so that Daniel could still truly say he did not understand the vision.[1] He was still in doubt about the time, which had been made so prominent. He begins to pray, as recorded in chapter 9; and while still in supplication, Gabriel again appears with the information that he has returned to impart "skill and understanding." Then bidding Daniel to "understand the matter, and consider the vision," he begins the explanation with reference to the time by saying, "Seventy weeks are determined upon thy people and upon thy holy city," etc. It is evident that these seventy weeks must be a part of the 2300 days of the vision, or else the commission to make Daniel understand the vision failed, and Gabriel's allusion to it before beginning his discourse had no meaning. One of the definitions of the original word rendered "determined" is "to cut off." Seventy weeks, then, or 490 days, were "cut off" from the 2300 days, and the time of their beginning clearly marked by the words: —

> Know therefore and understand, that from the going forth of the commandment to restore and to build Jerusalem unto the Messiah the Prince shall be *seven weeks*, and *threescore and two weeks*. . . . And he shall confirm the covenant with many for *one week*.[2]

Here we have the seventy weeks divided into three shorter periods, $7+62+1=70$ weeks. It

[1] Dan. 8:27.   [2] Dan. 9:25-27.

will not be necessary to our object to dwell at great length on these various subdivisions with their respective events; for our chief concern now is to find when the whole period begun, in order to see where the 2300 days will end. But the seventy weeks are simply the first part of the longer period, and therefore they begin at the same point, although of course the closing dates are different.

When did the commandment go forth to restore and build Jerusalem? All will remember that under Nebuchadnezzar, Jerusalem was destroyed, and some of the people carried captive to Babylon. After seventy years, Cyrus the Persian gave permission for the temple to be rebuilt, and the work was begun, as recorded in Ezra 1-4. Then for a time the work was stopped; but it was resumed by permission of Darius, as related in chapter 6. Still another more liberal grant was made by Artaxerxes to Ezra, as told in chapter 7. The combined effect of these three decrees is specially mentioned as completing God's commandment in the matter: "And they builded, and finished it, according to the commandment of the God of Israel, and according to the commandment of Cyrus, and Darius, and Artaxerxes."[1]

Many fail to get the true date for the beginning of the seventy weeks and 2300 days, because they do not see that it took all three of these kings to issue the command as described in the prophecy, and that nothing further was required. Some make

---
[1] Ezra 6:14, last part.

the mistake of reckoning from the proclamation of Cyrus in 536 B. C.; and others go forward to the time of Nehemiah in 445 B. C. Both these dates are wrong; for Cyrus alone did not fulfil the command of God as contemplated in the prophecy, and the permission to Nehemiah was nothing more than a confirmation of what had before been accorded to Ezra. Hence the threefold decree, to fulfil the prophecy, must date from the seventh year of Artaxerxes, when the royal grant was made. This was in the year 457 B. C., as shown in the margin of the Bible at the beginning of chapter 7. Five months of that year had passed before Ezra reached Jerusalem, and some little time more must have elapsed before he could begin the work which marked the beginning of this prophetic period. Thus there were approximately $456\frac{1}{2}$ years from that time to the opening of the Christian era, A. D. 1.

Now we have found the starting-point — about the middle of 457 B. C. This date not only marks the beginning of the "seventy weeks," but it also fixes the beginning of the "2300 days," of which the seventy weeks were a part. We need only to add the 2300 days to this date to ascertain the time when they end.

A DAY FOR A YEAR.

Before proceeding to our final conclusion, we pause a moment to remark that in prophecy time is frequently used in a symbolic sense. In symbolic language small objects represent larger ones. In the vision of Daniel 8, a "ram" was the symbol of "Media and Persia," the "goat" of Grecia," etc. Symbolic time is represented on a similarly reduced scale. In this case a "day" is used to represent a literal year. This law of symbols is clearly stated in Eze. 4 : 6 and Num. 14 : 34, and it is well known and generally recognized by Bible students.

Therefore the 2300 "days" represent 2300 years — "each day for a year." The "seventy weeks," or 490 days, are 490 literal years. We then have 2300 years to add to the date 456½ B. C. in order to find where the period ends. It reaches to the middle of 1844 A. D.; for 456½ years B. C. and 1843½ years A. D. make 2300, the whole period. Therefore we have found the end of the period which was to elapse before the sanctuary should be cleansed — *1844* is the time, more than half a century in the past; and the cleansing of the sanctuary is now in progress in heaven. Solemn and important truth! The great antitypical day of atonement is now upon us, much of its time has already gone, and the close of the work of Christ as priest draws near. In the earthly sanctuary the cleansing occupied but one day in the year; and as that was an "example and shadow of heavenly things," we may know that the work of cleansing the true sanctuary will also be comparatively short. No date is given to tell when it will close, and the end will come like a snare on the thoughtless world.

Before leaving this subject, a few words further concerning the "seventy weeks" will be in order. That this period is a key to unlock the prophecy concerning the "two thousand and three hundred days" is clearly shown by the angel's reference to the former vision. The connection between the two periods is that the former is the *first part of the latter*, a portion "cut off" and explained, in order that the whole may be understood. The seventy weeks being the first part of the 2300 days, the beginning of the seventy weeks must of necessity mark the beginning of the 2300 days. This, as before mentioned, was $456\frac{1}{2}$ B. C., when Artaxerxes issued his part of the threefold "commandment," as stated in Ezra 6 : 14. Reckoning from that date, the 2300 days (or years) would necessarily end $1843\frac{1}{2}$ years A. D. Nothing more is required to settle conclusively the time for the cleansing of the sanctuary to begin.

Reckoning from the same date, the 490 days ended in the year 34 A. D., and marked the time during which the Lord would still spare the unbelieving nation of Israel. All their national privileges, therefore, ended with the close of the seventy weeks in A. D. 34. Several definite steps in the history of that people are indicated by subdivisions in the period allotted to them. Thus "seven weeks," or forty-nine years, were assigned for the restoration of Jerusalem and the return of Israel and Judah from the captivity in Babylon. Sixty-two weeks more, or sixty-nine from the commencement — 483 years in all — reached to the appearing of "the Messiah the Prince," in the year A. D. 27.[1] "Messiah" in Hebrew and "Christ" in Greek mean the same thing, namely, the "*Anointed One.*" Jesus was anointed "*with the Holy Ghost*"[2] at his baptism by John[3] in the "fifteenth year of the reign of Tiberius,"[4] which was A. D. 27. Thus we have the strongest confirmatory proof of the correctness of our date $456\frac{1}{2}$ B. C. For, observe that sixty-nine weeks, or 483 years, from that point end in A. D. 27, and by independent evidence we learn that this was the exact time when Jesus was anointed as Christ the Messiah. Hence we are brought to the opening of Christ's public ministry by the termination of the sixty-nine weeks.

Only "one week" remained, the seventieth and last — seven more years for national Israel. The last supreme effort in behalf of a guilty people was yet to be made. For half of this time the "King of Israel" in person proclaimed the gospel in word and deed. Three and a half years he went in and out before them, and then he was crucified, fulfilling the prediction of Dan. 9 : 27 : "And in the

---

[1] Read carefully chapters 8 and 9 of the prophecy of Daniel. For a full explanation of the sanctuary and 2300 days, see "Looking unto Jesus," by U. Smith, published by the Review and Herald Publishing Co., Battle Creek, Mich.
[2] Acts 10 : 38.   [3] Matt. 3 : 13-16.   [4] Luke 3 : 1.

midst of the week, he shall cause the sacrifice and the oblation to cease." He was the great Sacrifice, the Lamb of God, and when he cried, "It is finished," the typical service in the earthly sanctuary ended forever, and the "veil of the temple was rent in twain from the top to the bottom," to mark the exact moment when the old covenant ended, and the new covenant was ratified by the shedding of his blood.

During all his ministry, Christ had taught them that only by him could they obey the law of God, commanded when the old covenant was made at Sinai. They must permit the law to be written on their hearts, and not trust to human power or natural birth. For three and a half years longer did the disciples continue to labor for the people of Israel, thus filling up the last week of years.[1] At last the cup of Israel's apostasy was filled, and they were left in blindness, while the apostles turned to the Gentiles, that out of all nations God might take a people for his name; and "so all Israel shall be saved." The overthrow and the perpetual scattering of the Jewish people is described in the closing words of the chapter: —

And for the overspreading of abominations he shall make it desolate, even until the consummation, and that determined shall be poured upon the desolator.[2]

There is no occasion for doubt as to what is intended by the words "desolator" and "abomi-

---

[1] Heb. 9:3. [2] Dan. 9:27, margin

THE SANCTUARY.

nations" that make "desolate." Christ refers to this very prediction in warning his disciples of the coming destruction of Jerusalem: —

> When ye therefore shall see the *abomination of desolation*, spoken of by Daniel the prophet, stand in the holy place (whoso readeth, let him understand:), then let them which be in Judea flee into the mountains.[1] And when ye shall see *Jerusalem compassed with armies*, then know that the destruction thereof is nigh.[2]

All are aware that the armies of Rome under Titus did surround and destroy Jerusalem A. D. 70, thus accomplishing the exact thing foretold by Daniel and by Christ. This desolation, the prophecy asserts, shall continue until the "consummation," and that determined upon the "desolator" shall be poured out. As Rome is the "desolator," we inquire what judgment has God determined upon that cruel power in the "consummation"? Under the symbol of a "little horn," the last division of Rome, the papacy, is described in Daniel 7, and her portion in the consummation is revealed: —

> But the judgment shall sit, and they shall take away his dominion, to *consume and to destroy it unto the end.*[3] The judgment was set, and the books were opened. I beheld then because of the voice of the great words which the horn spake; *I beheld even till the beast was slain, and his body destroyed, and given to the burning flame.*[4]

This is the desolation that comes on Rome, the desolator of Israel, in the consummation. Already

[1] Matt. 24 : 15, 16. [2] Luke 21 : 20.
[3] Dan. 7 : 26. [4] Dan. 7 : 10, 11.

the judgment is set, in the deciding work now going on in the sanctuary's cleansing, which began in 1844. Already, then, the desolation of Rome is near; for the next step following the judgment is to consume his *dominion.* The last vestige of the temporal dominion of the papacy ended in 1870, when Victor Emmanuel, king of Italy, confiscated the states of the Church, and the pope has since remained a voluntary prisoner in the Vatican, bewailing his desolation.

In that same year, 1870, the papal doctrine of "infallibility" was promulgated. Are not these the "great words" Daniel heard the horn speak while the judgment was in progress before the Ancient of Days? Then the next thing is to consume that apostate power in the "burning flame." This is the consummation determined upon the desolator. Paul calls him the "man of sin," "that wicked," "whom the Lord shall consume with the spirit of his mouth, and shall destroy with the brightness of his coming."[1] The papal system is the culmination of antichristian power, and embraces the only "Antichrist" of the last days. His consummation is determined, and the Eastern Question will close his career.

This application of the prophecy concerning the last week of the seventy is so Scriptural and consistent that it is painful to mention the perverse disposition often shown to deny it, in order tenaciously to maintain a contrary theory. There are

---

[1] 2 Thess. 2:3, 8.

some who, in the most arbitrary and illogical manner, entirely disconnect the seventieth week from the sixty-nine weeks, and carry it forward some eighteen hundred years, and then invent a series of impossible persons and events in a future time to meet certain conditions which are supposed to be coming. Rarely is a more open attempt made to wrest Scripture in conformity to a mere opinion. With some slight variations, all the advocates of this theory admit that the sixty-nine weeks ended about the time of the first advent; and yet they claim that the seventieth week has not yet commenced. Over eighteen hundred years are inserted without the least shadow of excuse, in order to make the events of the last week come in to support their theory of a future restoration of Israel.

Not one of these persons can point to an intimation in the prophecy that the seventieth week should not immediately follow the sixty-ninth. The fact that it is one of the "seventy," instead of standing entirely alone, would of itself be sufficient evidence that it was connected with them as part of the series, even though it cannot be shown that the events took place in that age. But no such difficulty exists. The fulfilment of every event mentioned is easily identified in well-known and important events of the few years subsequent to the appearing of the Messiah. His crucifixion in the midst of the week, and the rejection of the

Hebrew nation at its close, exactly correspond with the prophecy. The later desolation of the city by Rome is a historical fact of universal knowledge. And yet the advocates of this theory will make the sixty-nine weeks extend to the very time when Christ came into the world, and then pass over every event in his ministry; pay no attention to his death; make no mention of the new covenant, which Paul asserts was made with Israel; disregard the rejection of the Jewish nation; leave out everything connected with the destruction of Jerusalem and the scattering of the Jews; pass by Rome and all matters for eighteen centuries as too trivial for notice, in order to bolster up their baseless theory concerning the return of the Jews, Israel, etc.

To carry out this idea, they have to manufacture a new "desolator," some unheard-of "Antichrist," some awful monster of oppression, who is yet to arise, and make a covenant with the Jews, and then turn about and destroy them. Some look for another Napoleon to fulfil these frightful dreams; others surmise that some Russian autocrat will be the man; still others think the long-dead Nero of Rome will live again to accomplish their predictions; and lastly some unknown Syrian king is expected by a few. None of these crude, fanciful, extravagant ideas will be entertained, if the easy, natural method of connecting the last week with the preceding ones is adopted. True, it will destroy an argument used to uphold the future restoration of national Israel; but that theory is not really strengthened by such an unnatural thing as interjecting two millenniums between the sixty-ninth and seventieth weeks.

At every step in its development, there is harmony in the divine plan. We have now examined briefly the sanctuary and its cleansing. At each unfolding of the subject have appeared facts corresponding with what we have found from a multitude of sources; namely, that we have reached the "last days;" that the work of Christ in the pardon of sin is all done in heaven before his second advent to this earth; that he will not restore Jerusalem nor Palestine; that the Jews will not be gathered again; that the dream of a future age for the conversion of the world is a monstrous fable, invented by the father of lies to deceive a careless world and a sleeping church; that the fulness of the Gentiles is about come; that true Israel will soon be numbered and saved; and that even now their cases are passing in review in the true sanctuary.

It is unnecessary to say more to convince any one who reads thus far that we are rapidly reaching a crisis for which the mass of mankind are unprepared. Everything in this world, both political and religious, is tending toward the solution of the Eastern Question. Is it in connection with that grim horror that the hopes of a deluded world will be blasted? While looking to Jerusalem as the center from which universal peace on earth is to proceed, will it be the scene of the most terrible war ever known among men? One thing is certain; true Israel will not look to the East for the fulfilment of their hopes. They look above; they look not to old Jerusalem, but to the New Jerusalem; not to Palestine, but to the new earth. While the closing work in the sanctuary is going forward, they will be seeking meekness and righteousness, so that their "sins may be blotted out, when the times of refreshing shall come from the presence of the Lord; and he shall send Jesus Christ, which before was preached unto you; whom the heaven must receive until the times of restitution of all things, which God hath spoken by the mouth of all his holy prophets since the world began."[1]

[1] Acts 3 : 19-21.

Chapter Nine.

THE KINGDOM OF CHRIST.

PROMINENT among the promises of Israel are those that relate to the kingdom of Christ, and his reign on the throne of David. Owing to a misunderstanding of the term "Israel," also to wrong views of the "promised land" and the sanctuary, many think that Christ will yet establish his throne at Jerusalem, in the land of Palestine, and that his kingdom will be gradually extended thence, until, during a millennium of peace, all the world will be brought in loving homage to his feet.

If the theory just stated is correct, the Eastern Question must be involved in it; for at present a false religion is held by the government in control of Jerusalem and the land of Judea. In fact, many anticipate that when the Turk is subdued, the world will have peace, so that the nations can "beat their swords into plowshares, and their spears into pruning hooks," and thus the millennium will be brought in. Some of these conclusions have already been disproved. We have found that the Hebrew people will never be a nation again, and that the promises do not apply to them.

It has also been shown that true Israel, to whom the promises are given, will not receive their inheritance in the present world, but in a "world to come." Further, we have learned that Christ is now finishing his work as priest in the heavenly sanctuary, which brings the close of probation to all mankind. Finally, that the "fulness of the Gentiles" and that of true Israel occur at the same time, but that one is the opposite of the other. These facts alone would show that Christ's kingdom will not be set up on this earth. But there are independent promises which pertain to this special topic, and these will repay examination.

In order to remove all doubt, let it be distinctly stated that our position is that the reign of Christ on David's throne is to be in the new earth, and not on any part of this present world. One of the most popular opposite views was forcibly and eloquently expressed by the honored president of the National Woman's Christian Temperance Union, Miss Frances E. Willard, in her address before the annual convention of 1887, at Nashville, Tenn., and reported in the *Union Signal*, their official organ, under date of Dec. 1, 1887, as follows: —

> The Woman's Christian Temperance Union, local, State, national, and world-wide, has one vital, organic thought, one all-absorbing purpose, one undying enthusiasm, and that is that Christ shall be *this world's king;* — yea, verily, THIS WORLD'S KING in its realm of cause and effect, — king of its courts, its camp, its commerce, — king of its colleges and

cloisters,— king of its customs and its constitutions. . . . The kingdom of Christ must enter the realm of law through the gateway of politics. . . . We pray Heaven to give them [the old political parties] no rest . . . until they shall . . . swear an oath of allegiance to Christ in politics, and march in one great army up to the polls to worship God. . . . There is just one question that every Christian ought to ask: What is the relation of this party, this platform, this candidate, *to the setting up of Christ's kingdom on the earth ?* How does my vote relate to the Lord's prayer ? . . . Our prayers are prophets, and predict this day of glad deliverance as being at the door. . . . *To-day Christ sits over against the ballot-box, as of old he sat over against the treasury, and judges men by what they cast therein.*

Hundreds of thousands of earnest Christian women all over the world tacitly, if not openly, endorse the policy and principles set forth in the foregoing extract. So far as we know, Miss Willard does not advocate the idea that Christ will reign personally in this world, at Jerusalem or anywhere else. Probably her thought is that he will reign by proxy, and administer his law through some human organization. But others who expect the kingdom of Christ to be set up in this world teach that Christ will come in person, and begin his reign in Jerusalem, although they may differ with the plan proposed by the W. C. T. U. for bringing it about. Some look for the return of the Jews and the subjugation of the Turks as necessary preliminary steps. It is not the purpose in this work to discuss all or any of these various theories at much length; they are cited only as showing the wide-spread expectation that in some way Christ is to reign over the nations of this world.

Our first appeal for proof on this subject is to the words of Christ himself, before Pilate. "Art thou the King of the Jews?" is the direct question.

> Jesus answered: *My kingdom is not of this world.* If my kingdom were of this world, then would my servants fight, that I should not be delivered to the Jews; but now is my kingdom not from hence.[1]

Please compare this statement of the King with the quotation from the W. C. T. U. president. He declares that his kingdom is not of this world. She declares that he shall be this world's king. Both cannot be true. The issue between them is not one of method, but of fact. One organization may vote for it, another fight for it, and still another preach about it; but all of them together cannot succeed, for the simple reason that his "kingdom is not of this world." His throne will not be set up at Jerusalem, or at any other place in this world. All the "undying enthusiasm" of men and women will fail to change the eternal plan and purpose of God, as set forth so clearly in his word. This theory is one of the great delusions of the age, and is destined to bring infinite trouble and sorrow.

[1] John 18:33, 36.

A MONSTROUS FABLE.

Perhaps the reply will be made that Christ referred to moral condition instead of locality, and that the people will finally become so changed, either by politics and the ballot-box, or by the preaching of the gospel, that he will reign over a converted world. But we inquire, Where is the evidence of such a transformation? Does the Bible tell us of a time when the way to destruction will be so strait and narrow that none can find it, or at most but few, while the way to life will become so broad and easy that the multitude will walk therein? Does it say that before the harvest comes, all the tares will become wheat? Does it state that Christ's followers will become a vast majority, while the wicked will be only a "little flock"?

The entire Bible is squarely against the doctrine of a world's conversion. Common observation disproves it. Education is not religion. Civilization is not true Christianity. Culture is not conversion. The antediluvians had wealth; the people of Sodom had riches and leisure; the Hebrew nation had an imposing religious service; Greece and Rome had culture and power. To-day all these favorable circumstances are found in a portion of the world, but the possessors of these blessings are not made meek and contrite. That God has many true witnesses both in word and in deed, we are glad to maintain;

but that the mass of men are morally improving we doubt, and that the world will ever be converted we deny.

A MAGNIFICENT OFFER.

Returning to the subject of Christ's reigning in this world, we find another occasion when an "absorbing purpose" was manifested in this matter. Satan himself was determined that Christ should receive the kingdom of this world. To accomplish his design, he resorted to "politics." He made a most generous offer; first, he showed Christ all the kingdoms of this world and the glory of them, and then agreed to transfer his own title to all these possessions in return for a very small political favor; "just worship me, and all shall be yours." Never did wily candidate manifest greater concern for the suffering public, than was manifested on that occasion. Here was a bribe unequaled in the annals of time — not simply a "kingdom for a horse," but a world for a word. This opportunity was spurned with the stern command, "Get thee behind me, Satan." Only by the cross could he win the world — not the present world, but the "world to come." Only by that same cross can men to-day be won for the kingdom of Christ in that better land. Political methods will never prepare a single soul for that inheritance, nor install Christ as king. He will dwell in the humble, contrite heart which trembles at his word, but not in a heart which through political intrigues or governmental laws is forced into a hypocritical profession.

Satan is still the god of this world, and if he can now induce the people to receive the kingdom, it will be on the same terms held out to Christ. Let all who have "one organic thought" to make Christ this world's king, be careful lest they worship Satan in the attempt.

The claim may be put forth that while it would be inconsistent for Christ to receive the kingdom from Satan, his enemy and rival, it would be acceptable if presented as a voluntary endowment from his friends. In answer to this, notice the following scripture: —

> Then those men, when they had seen the miracle that Jesus did, said, This is of a truth that prophet that should come into the world. When Jesus therefore perceived that they would come and take him by force, *to make him a king, he departed again into a mountain himself alone.*[1]

Here was just such zeal as many now manifest. They were ready to crown Christ king of the world, while they would shut him out of their hearts. Ambition may lead to extraordinary exertions to win the world for Christ, and yet refuse to hear his word saying, "My kingdom is not of this world." In olden times, he left the professed friends who so mistook the nature of his work; will he not to-day leave any person or organization that persists in the same course? The whole

[1] John 6:14, 15.

theory is wrong. In the new earth Christ will have his kingdom, and Israel will then be "joint-heirs" with him. He is indeed "The King of the Jews," or "King of Israel;" but all are invited to become Israel, and share in the glory that belongs to the sons of God. "Whosoever will, let him come."

THE THRONE OF DAVID.

Much of the confusion existing on the subject of Christ's kingdom is due to another serious error; namely, a failure to distinguish between the present position of Christ on the Father's throne, and his future reign on his own throne. It may not be necessary to conclude that there are actually two separate thrones; but the fact that Christ reigns at two different times under changed conditions cannot be denied. One text directly bearing on this point will be sufficient: —.

To him that overcometh will I grant to sit with me in my throne, even as I also overcame, and am set down with my Father in his throne.[1]

For convenience in distinguishing these separate positions, we will call the present one the throne of the Father, and the future one the throne of Christ, or use equivalent expressions.

We are assured that when Christ ascended to heaven, he sat down at "the right hand of God."[2] His office while thus sitting with the Father is thus described: —

[1] Rev. 3:21.   [2] Mark 16:19.

Now of the things which we have spoken this is the sum : We have such an high priest, who is set on the right hand of the throne of the Majesty in the heavens; a minister of the sanctuary, and of the true tabernacle, which the Lord pitched, and not man.[1]

Christ is now a priest in the true sanctuary in heaven, at the right hand of God, fulfilling the Scripture, "Thou art a priest forever after the order of Melchisedec."[2] Concerning this man who was a type of Christ, we read that he was "king of Salem, priest of the most high God."[3] He was both king and priest, and so could represent the present work of Christ as both king and priest.

David was a mighty king, but he was not a priest. He was of the tribe of Judah, while to the tribe of Levi belonged the priesthood. Hence David could not be a type of Christ's present reign as priest. When the time comes for Christ to sit on David's throne, his work as priest will be done. There will be no priesthood on the throne of David, no offering of the sacrificial blood, no atonement in the sanctuary, no work of mediator or advocate. No one can be saved without Christ's ministry in these matters; hence it will be readily seen that probation will close when the change is made. No single sinner can be converted after Christ takes the throne of David; for there will then be no priest to bear his sins and make atonement for them. In view of this fact, we may be

[1] Heb. 8:1, 2. [2] Heb. 7:17. [3] Heb. 7:1.

devoutly thankful that no human power can make him king of this world; for that would close the destiny of all the race immediately. Can any one fail to see the terrible mistake of expecting the world to be converted after Christ begins his reign on David's throne?

We are not left to human deductions, however logical they may be; but the word of the Lord bears direct testimony as to what will take place when Christ leaves his present position and office as priest on the Father's throne: "*Then cometh the end*, when he shall have delivered up the kingdom to God, even the Father."[1] The "end" of what? — The end of his work as priest; the end of probation; the end of this present age; the end of all human kingdoms; the end of all who obey not the gospel. How strange that what the Lord calls the "end," men are expecting to be the "beginning" of a better age; the "beginning" of the millennium; the "beginning" of the world's conversion.

Evidence to show the true nature of Christ's kingdom and refute the false theories taught concerning it, is so abundant, that in citing it there may be danger of hiding the simple truth already so clearly seen. Go carefully over still another line. In Revelation we read: —

And the *seventh angel sounded;* and there were great voices in heaven, saying, The kingdoms of this world are

1 Cor. 15:24.

become the kingdoms of our Lord, and of his Christ; and he shall reign forever and ever.[1]

And again: —

But in the days of the voice of the *seventh angel, when he shall begin to sound*, the mystery of God should be finished, as he hath declared to his servants the prophets.[2]

Putting these two texts together, we see that *the mystery of God is finished*, and *Christ receives the kingdoms of this world*, at the *same time;* namely, under the sounding of the seventh angel. What is the "mystery of God"? An answer is found by comparing a few statements of the apostle Paul: —

Now to Him that is of power to stablish you according to my *gospel*, and the preaching of Jesus Christ, according to the *revelation of the mystery*, which was kept secret since the world began.[3]

Here we learn that the *gospel* is the *mystery*. The same fact is stated in other words: —

And for me, that utterance may be given unto me, that I may open my mouth boldly, to make known the *mystery of the gospel*.[4]

In another place Paul speaks of the "*mystery of his will.*" There can be no doubt that the "mystery of God" is the "will" of God, as manifested in the gospel. Now we can draw our conclusion; under the sounding of the seventh angel, the "mystery of God," the gospel, is finished; and at the same time the kingdoms of this world are

---

[1] Rev. 11 : 15.   [3] Rev. 10 : 7.   [4] Rom. 16 : 25.
[2] Eph. 6 : 19.

given to Christ; *the work of the gospel ends when Christ takes his kingdom.*

We invite the reader to trace with us another path which reaches the same point: —

I beheld till the thrones were cast down, and the Ancient of Days did sit; . . . the judgment was set, and the books were opened. . . . I saw in the night visions, and, behold, one like unto the Son of Man came with the clouds of heaven, and came to the Ancient of Days, and they brought him near before him. And there was given him dominion, and glory, and a kingdom, that all people, nations, and languages should serve him; his dominion is an everlasting dominion which shall not pass away, and his kingdom that which shall not be destroyed.[1]

Notice here that the *judgment precedes the coronation of Christ.* But the very purpose of the judgment is to decide the destiny of all men. There can be no reversal of its decisions; hence there can be no gospel work performed for sinners — no conversion for those pronounced "unholy" in that tribunal. But Christ comes to the Ancient of Days, the Father, as the "advocate" of all who have received his ministration as priest, and they are pronounced "holy." This completes the work of Christ in the true sanctuary on the throne of God, and he next receives the throne of David over the nations of earth. Only those who *now* receive Christ as king in their own hearts, and whose names he confesses in the work of cleansing the sanctuary, will share in the glory of his kingdom in the world to come. "*Now* is the accepted time;

[1] Dan. 7: 9-14.

behold, *now* is the day of salvation." There is no excuse for deception in this matter. Be not misled by any theory of a future age, where the conditions of salvation will be extended to the race.

THE NATIONS TO BE DESTROYED.

The evidence that instead of the world's *conversion*, its *destruction* will follow the setting up of Christ's kingdom, is ample and decisive. First notice the Father's words to the Son in psalm 110:—

> The Lord said unto my Lord, Sit thou at my right hand, until I make thine enemies thy footstool. The Lord shall send the rod of thy strength out of Zion; rule thou in the midst of thine enemies. Thy people shall be willing in the day of thy power. . . . The Lord hath sworn, and will not repent, Thou art a priest forever after the order of Melchisedec. The Lord at thy right hand shall strike through kings in the day of his wrath. He shall judge among the heathen, *he shall fill the places with the dead bodies;* he shall wound the heads over many countries.

Language has no meaning, if this is not a description of a terrible ruin. Again we read: —

> I will declare the decree: the Lord hath said unto me, Thou art my Son; this day have I begotten thee. Ask of me, and I shall give thee the heathen for thine inheritance, and the uttermost parts of the earth for thy possession. *Thou shalt break them with a rod of iron; thou shalt dash them in pieces like a potter's vessel.*[1]

Similar words are used in Revelation with an application which cannot be mistaken for the work of the gospel in converting men: —

[1] Ps. 2: 7-9.

And out of his mouth goeth a sharp sword, that with it he should smite the nations; and he shall rule them with a rod of iron: *and he treadeth the winepress of the fierceness and wrath of Almighty God.* And he hath on his vesture and on his thigh a name written, KING OF KINGS AND LORD OF LORDS.[1]

In the following verses a description is given of the dreadful slaughter which accompanies this terrible manifestation of divine wrath. And all this is involved in the change from Christ's office as priest to that of king.

This solemn lesson is taught in parable as well as in prophecy: —

And as they heard these things, he added and spake a parable, because he was nigh to Jerusalem, and because they thought that the kingdom of God should immediately appear. He said therefore, A certain nobleman went into a far country to receive for himself a kingdom, and to return. And he called his ten servants, and delivered them ten pounds, and said unto them, Occupy till I come. But his citizens hated him, and sent a message after him, saying, We will not have this man to reign over us. And it came to pass, that when he was returned, having received the kingdom, then he commanded these servants to be called unto him. . . . Those mine enemies, which would not that I should reign over them, *bring hither, and slay them before me.*[2]

Probably no one will dispute the application of this parable to Christ and his enemies when he comes into possession of the kingdom.

The parable of the wheat and tares in Matthew 13 teaches the same thing. Both grow together

[1] Rev. 19: 15, 16. [2] Luke 19: 11-27.

till the harvest, and the harvest is the end of the world. Then —

> The Son of Man shall send forth his angels, and they shall gather out of his kingdom all things that offend, and them which do iniquity; and shall cast them into a furnace of fire; there shall be wailing and gnashing of teeth. Then shall the righteous shine forth as the sun in the kingdom of their Father. Who hath ears to hear, let him hear.[1]

Certainly these texts do not teach the conversion of the world. The unmistakable conclusion to be drawn from them is that Christ's enemies, the finally impenitent, will all be destroyed at his coming.

Reader, Christ will not establish his throne on this earth, and reign over a mixed population of saints and sinners, thus converting the world. His kingdom will be in the world to come, after all that do evil are cut off, and only the "meek shall inherit the earth." The testimony on this subject is conclusive. When you utter the Lord's prayer, asking that his kingdom shall come and his will be done in earth as it is in heaven, may you truly understand the request, and worship him in *spirit* and in *truth*.

GENERAL REMARKS.

In tracing the Eastern Question thus far, we have found much to encourage interest in the Bible doctrine on this subject. No discord appears between the people, the place, the time, and the manner in which the promises of God are to be

[1] Matt. 13:41-43.

fulfilled. Such harmony on diverse lines and in independent texts is the sure accompaniment of truth. Do not confound the work of Christ on the Father's throne with something to be done on his own throne. Do not confound true Israel with national distinctions, and do not mistake promises to be fulfilled in the world to come for something to be done in this present world. In the crisis which is approaching, nothing but a correct understanding of these matters can keep any one from the ruin to come when the Eastern Question is finally settled. In succeeding chapters we will learn this more clearly.

Chapter Ten.

THE DOOM OF TURKEY.

THE Eastern Question centers in Turkey, but it involves the world. Turkey has long been known as the "Sick Man of the East," and one of the anomalies of the situation is that a government derisively termed the "Sick Man" should be able to keep the other European nations such anxious watchers by his bedside, not as loving friends, soothing his closing hours, but as interested beneficiaries in his mortgaged estate, seeking to realize as large a share as possible when foreclosure is made, and his estate is torn into fragments by rival claimants. Turkey is the "bone of contention" about which the other powers are growling. To that point all eyes are turned.

The Turkish dominions include Palestine and Jerusalem, once the home of the Hebrew nation, and believed by many to be the place where Christ will establish his kingdom on the throne of David. Thus the fate of Turkey is a subject of deep concern to the religious world. Recent events in that direction indicate that a crisis cannot long be delayed, and all dread the uncertain result of decisive action to stop the horrors already in progress. Extravagant theories abound, and definite dates are set, when it is conjectured that the climax for good or evil will come. If ever an utterance from the Lord was needed, it is now, to bring harmony out of these jarring discords. We make no attempts on the lines that have been mentioned; we have no figures to present; no prophetic period reaches to a later date than 1844, when the 2300 days of Dan. 8 : 14 ended, and the cleansing of the heavenly sanctuary was begun. But may we not find in the Bible clear and decisive information, without falling into the error so often witnessed of straining a text to fit a theory? Thus far we have found the Scriptures harmonious. Let us then listen still further to the words of inspiration.

No reader of God's word will forget that ancient nations are frequently mentioned by name in the prophetic writings. Babylon, Egypt, Assyria, Persia, Grecia, Judea, and others are familiar Bible words, and the predictions concerning each have been accurately fulfilled. More modern nations, like Rome and its ten divisions, embracing many European states, are clearly represented by various symbols. May we not therefore expect some mention to be made of Turkey, the stronghold of a false religion, and an important factor in the welfare and peace of mankind? The modern name "Turkey" is not found in the Bible; but the government, territory, and people are there described.

Prophetic expositors are agreed that Mohammedanism, which had its rise in the wastes of the Arabian desert, is symbolized in Revelation 9 by smoke that arose out of the bottomless pit; and the rude Saracen warriors, by devastating hordes of locusts. These swarming myriads were finally consolidated into governmental form by Othman, from whom the title Ottoman Empire is derived. Under this and subsequent leaders, they became a mighty power, finally subjugating the Eastern Empire of Rome, including a portion of Europe, with the city of Constantinople, and much of Western Asia with the important historical city of Jerusalem. The prophecy alludes to this conquest in Rev. 9 : 14, by the name of the chief river of that region, the Euphrates.

For more complete information concerning the recent history of Turkey, we turn to Daniel 11. This is a literal prophecy of great interest, where, under the title "king of the north," the same power is represented. To show clearly that this is the correct application, let us consider a few points in the prophecy where the term is used. From Dan. 10 : 1 we learn that this information was given by an angel, evidently Gabriel, in the third year of Cyrus, king of Persia. From that period the prophecy is continued in chapter 11. After stating that he had ministered during the reign of a former king, Darius, the angel turns to the future: —

And now will I show thee the truth. Behold, there shall stand up yet three kings in Persia; and the fourth shall be far richer than they all: and by his strength through his riches he shall stir up all against the realm of Grecia.[1]

The expression to "stand up," as used in this verse, means to come to the throne, to reign in the kingdom. The same expression occurs several times in the prophecy, and is always used in the same sense. From history we learn the names of the four kings which successively followed Cyrus on the Persian throne: Cambyses, Smerdis, Darius, and Xerxes. The last is called Ahasuerus in the Bible account in the book of Esther. His famous expedition against Grecia, with an army of over 5,000,000, is recorded by the historian Herodotus. This huge invasion was successfully repelled by the mere handful of Grecian heroes, and the account of it forms one of the most thrilling chapters in the record of this world's strife. Every schoolboy knows the story.

Having introduced the kingdom of Grecia, the prophecy now proceeds with that rising power under Alexander: —

And a mighty king shall stand up, that shall rule with great dominion, and do according to his will.[2]

This tells the entire story of Alexander's conquests. The next verse records his fall: —

And when he shall stand up, his kingdom shall be broken, and shall be divided toward the four winds of heaven; and

---

[1] Dan. 11:2.   [2] Dan. 11:3.

not to his posterity, nor according to his dominion which he ruled; for his kingdom shall be plucked up, even for others besides those.

Soon after Alexander's death, in the prime of life and the fulness of power, the territory over which he had ruled was divided among his four leading generals. Thus the kingdom was divided into four parts "toward the four winds of heaven." One portion was toward the north, and one toward the south. These two portions are repeatedly mentioned in the rest of the chapter; but nothing is said of the others, toward the west and toward the east, for the latter were soon incorporated in the dominion of the "king of the north."

From this it will be seen that the power called the "king of the north" must be the one which occupies the northern portion of Alexander's empire. Many mistake here, thinking Russia is the nation specified. It is true that Russia is a northern power, and is connected with the Eastern Question; but its territory was not included in Alexander's dominion, which was divided according to the prophecy, and as we must be guided by the prophecy in looking for the territory and government indicated, Russia cannot be the "king of the north."

Turkey now occupies the northern division of the Grecian Empire; therefore Turkey is the "king of the north" when the prophecy comes down to modern times. Passing over the various conflicts mentioned in the chapter, we notice particularly verse 41, where the "king of the north" is seen in possession of "the glorious land," evidently referring to Palestine, which, as all know, is now a part of the sultan's realm. The next two verses speak of the partial conquest of Egypt, elsewhere in this prophecy called "the king of the south."

> But tidings out of the east and out of the north shall trouble him: therefore he shall go forth with great fury to destroy, and utterly to make away many.[1]

Here is additional evidence that the "king of the north" is Turkey, and not Russia. Notice that "tidings out of the north" trouble the "king of the north." Now if Russia were the "king of the north," how could tidings out of the north trouble him? There is no hostile power north of Russia, there can be none; for the Russian possessions extend to the Arctic Ocean. Therefore no tidings from the north of Russia can ever trouble Russia. But with Turkey all is different. Here, as already shown, is the country called "the king of the north" in the primary division, which must govern the use of the term; and from Turkish soil we look north to see the source whence tidings of trouble come. Our eye immediately rests on Russia. Everybody knows that from that source disquieting tidings are wafted to Constantinople on every breeze. Russia greatly desires Constantinople and the territory now held by Turkey. These are facts of common knowledge and comment all

[1] Dan. 11 : 44.

over the world; therefore any direct proof on this point is superfluous. Indeed, the Eastern Question has grown up out of this desire on the part of Russia and the unwillingness of the other powers of Europe to have it gratified. As a natural result, complications and jealousies arise.

Harassed by his enemies on all sides, the Turk, according to the prophecy, goes "forth with great fury to destroy and utterly to make away many." If this refers to a war declared against his troublesome neighbors, the "Crimean War" is an example of reckless wrath on the part of Turkey; for had not England and France interposed in his behalf, his destruction would have terminated his folly.

Only one result seems possible under the present circumstances of Turkish atrocities in the East: England and the other powers will no longer maintain the cause of Turkey against Russia, and the Turk will soon be driven from Europe. Already this course is agitated and recommended as the only solution to the difficulties. It needs no prophetic eye to see that Turkish days in Europe are about numbered, not only in the plan of God, but in the course of human events. Driven from Constantinople, where will the sultan take up his abode? Jerusalem is the most available place in his Asiatic possessions, and thither he will go. This is made sure by the next verse of the prophecy: "And he shall plant the tabernacles of his palace between the seas in the glorious holy mountain." Jerusalem, between the Dead Sea and the Mediterranean, is the place of the glorious holy mountain, Mount Zion. Therefore it seems certain that the last stand of the Turkish power will be at Jerusalem.

One more statement of the divine messenger will close the story of Turkey in prophecy: "Yet he shall come to his end, and none shall help him."[1] In vain he seeks shelter at Jerusalem, the "holy city." Those who have hitherto helped him, "help him" no more, and he comes to an "end." This is the doom of Turkey. Its reign of lust and murder is to "end." Its false religion, issuing like "smoke out of the bottomless pit," will ascend up as "smoke" before the gale. Jerusalem will be the scene of its final ruin. While the cross of Jesus of Nazareth, borne in sorrow and shame from Jerusalem's gate to Calvary, will stand forever, the crescent of Mohammed will sink forever beneath the walls of that same apostate city. The final slaughter of the wicked will take place where once the Lamb of God was led to the slaughter. O Jerusalem, many have been thy woes since that dreadful day when thy people cried, "His blood be on us and on our children;" but more fearful still will be thy doom in the final battle of the "day of the Lord."

We pause a moment before continuing the prophecy to remark that the Bible does not give

[1] Dan. 11:45.

the exact date when these events will take place. While all must realize that the end of the Turk is near, we need not be surprised if the present violent agitation is calmed, and that a little longer matters go on in the old way. Should this be the case, it will not in the least disprove the prophecy, nor overthrow the argument and conclusions based thereon. All we claim is, that sooner or later these things will be done as set forth, and that present indications make it at least probable that the end of Turkey is near.

MICHAEL THE PRINCE.

The prophecy we have considered does not close with Daniel 11, but is continued into chapter 12. Our last view was the "end" of Turkey. Now we turn to notice the condition of other nations as set forth in the next verse. The first sentence is, "And at that time shall Michael stand up." The "time" referred to is when Turkey's "end" comes. Something else occurs in connection with that scene. *Michael* then stands up. And who is Michael? He is spoken of by Gabriel in Dan. 10: 13, as "Michael [margin, "the first"], one of the chief princes;" and in verse 21 as "Michael your prince." In chapter 12: 1, after saying that "Michael shall stand up," he is described as "the great prince which standeth for the children of thy people." Turning to Rev. 12: 7, we learn that Michael was commander of the host in heaven which fought against the dragon, or Satan. In Jude 9 he is called the "archangel," who disputed with the devil about the body of Moses.

All these expressions point to a being higher than angels in might and authority. In other words, he must be the Son of God. Christ is indeed the "great prince;" he is the "chief prince." He is the one to "stand" for true Israel — Daniel's "people"— and make atonement for them in the heavenly sanctuary; he is the leader in the war against Satan; he has the power of life, and therefore could raise Moses from the dead, notwithstanding the devil's protest; he is the archangel; he is the "Lord himself," who "shall descend from heaven with a shout, with the voice of the archangel, and with the trump of God; and the dead in Christ shall rise first."[1] Summing up these statements, we learn that the Lord is the archangel, and that the archangel is Michael; therefore the Lord is Michael, or Michael is Christ.

Thus we learn that at the time when the "king of the north," or Turkey, shall come to his end at Jerusalem, with none to help him, Christ shall "stand up" in heaven. We have already noticed that in this prophecy the expression "stand up" denotes kingly authority, taking the throne to reign. We quote the words again: "Behold, there shall *stand up* yet three kings in Persia;" "and a mighty king shall *stand up;*" "and when he shall *stand up*, his kingdom shall be broken."[2]

---

[1] 1 Thess. 4:16.   [2] Dan. 11:2-4.

In all these cases the term is readily understood to refer to the time when these earthly potentates came to the throne. It means the same when it is applied to Christ, or Michael. When he "*stands up*," it will be to receive from his Father the kingdom, the throne of David, in the world to come. As shown in a preceding chapter, Christ is now our high priest on the throne of his Father. But when this prophecy is fulfilled, and Michael "stands up," or takes his own throne, it will conclude his work as priest and advocate on the Father's throne, where he now ministers pardon and strength to all who seek his favor; it will close the probation of the human race, seal the eternal destiny of all men by the decree of the judgment, and bring the dashing in pieces of the nations like a potter's vessel.

A TIME OF TROUBLE.

In harmony with the conclusions drawn from other sources, we now present direct and positive assertion from the prophecy; for the next statement, speaking of the time when this change is made in Christ's ministry, is, "And there shall be a time of trouble, such as never was since there was a nation even to that same time."[1] Notice that this time of trouble comes on the *nations*. This text does not speak of the same time nor the same class of people mentioned in the "great tribulation" of Matt. 24 : 21. The latter refers to the

[1] Dan. 12:1.

true people of God, the elect, during the persecutions of the Dark Ages, when the church fled into the wilderness for 1260 years. The time of trouble spoken of in Dan. 12 : 1 is an entirely different matter, and is still future; for it comes when "the king of the north" reaches his end, and when Christ takes the throne of David. This, too, comes upon the wicked nations, while the same verse says the people of God are "delivered." This is the time for the "fulness of the Gentiles" and also for the "fulness" of true Israel. There is no necessity for confounding these things.

Our investigation has led to a conclusion of solemn import. A chapter of awful horror is yet to be written in the history of this world, and then "The End" may be placed on the last page, and the volume closed. No previous time of trouble — not even the flood, nor the destruction of ancient Jerusalem — can compare with the one to be ushered in when Michael stands up. God in mercy reveals these things in advance, in order that all may flee to the city of refuge. The present and approaching disasters of Turkey are the dying cries of the "Sick Man" to a perishing world. His end brings the end to all the nations, the end of the day of salvation, the end of the harvest. While the angry nations are demanding the immediate punishment of Turkey, and the close of the Eastern Question, which will engulf the earth in ruin, God is still holding the winds of strife a little longer, so that the world may be warned, and the remnant of true Israel gathered out and sealed for his kingdom. While so many religious teachers, no doubt with honest intentions in most cases at least, are bending every energy to make Christ this world's king, and so close the door of hope to every unconverted person, Jesus is still waiting, in order that he may finish the "mystery of God," "cleanse the sanctuary," and "stand" as advocate for his people Israel before the Father's throne. Then, when the time of trouble bursts upon the nations, his "people shall be delivered, every one that shall be found written in the book."

Reader, is your name in the Lamb's book of life? Are you one of the Israel of God? Will the Great Prince stand for you in the judgment? Will he deliver you in the time of trouble? Will you sit on his throne in the world to come? Let the mutterings of the coming storm over Turkey and the Eastern Question cause us to seek shelter beneath the wings of Him who says, "Come unto me, and I will give you rest." It is not fanaticism which points out these dangers to a careless world and a lukewarm church. These are not the vagaries of human theories, but the truth of the living God has been presented. Line upon line we have traced the very words of inspiration; and the conclusions in each case are the logical results of the facts set forth in the Scriptures, and in perfect harmony every voice from Genesis to Revelation attests that here is the solid rock, the sure foundation, for the world to come.

ARMAGEDDON.

Still another portion of Scripture particularly describing the doom of Turkey and the accompanying ruin to all the world, is found in Rev. 16 : 12–21. In this connection we will dwell only on those features which have already been discussed, reserving others to a later chapter. Attention has been called to the fact that the rise of the Ottoman Empire was symbolized in Revelation 9 by the great river Euphrates. In chapter 16 : 12 is sketched the decline of the same government, represented by the same symbol: —

> And the sixth angel poured out his vial upon the great river Euphrates; and the water thereof was dried up, that the way of the kings of the East might be prepared.

This application is so consistent, and so generally acknowledged, that it is unnecessary to offer further proof. Here, then, is Turkey, particularly in its Asiatic possessions, watered by the Euphrates River. Waters, when taken as a symbol, denote people, nations, etc.[1] Therefore the drying up of the river Euphrates must indicate the gradual shrinking of the sultan's dominions. Already the European possessions of Turkey have dwindled away to nearly one third their original area, and still the process goes on, and the day cannot be far distant when it will no longer have a foothold

[1] Rev. 17 : 15.

on the soil of Europe. Then the sultan will be obliged to move over into Asia, and this is what the prophecy of Daniel affirms that he will do. Even then the consumption will go on until the territory watered by the Euphrates will also be wrenched from his grasp, and he will have come to his end. This absorption of the Turkish possessions will arouse the hostility or cupidity of all nations, and their respective military forces, now training for that very emergency, will be called into action. It is distinctly stated in the prophecy that the drying up of the Euphrates prepares the way for the kings of the *East*. This is the Eastern Question, and the crisis will surely come.

From verse 14 we learn that the whole world will be involved. "The kings of the earth and of the *whole world*" will thus be gathered to Palestine "to the battle of that great day of God Almighty." "And he gathered them together into a place called in the Hebrew tongue Armageddon." This name is applied to the region called the plain of Esdraelon, watered by the river Kishon, and overlooked by the hills of Megiddo. Here is one of the famous battle-fields of ancient times; and here on its blood-soaked soil will be gathered the warlike nations of the world in battle array. Here, amid the "wreck of matter and the crash of worlds," will be fought the battle of the great day of God Almighty, and the nations will be broken in shivers like a potter's vessel. Like chaff from the summer threshing-floor will the kingdoms of this world be blown away by the gale, in order that this earth may be made new for the kingdom of Christ, when he shall reign over his people Israel on the throne of David. This is the "fulness of the Gentiles" mentioned by Paul; the "time of trouble" mentioned by Daniel; the "beating of the floods" on the house founded on the sand, mentioned by Christ; the "whirlwind" mentioned by Isaiah. It is not with pleasure that these fearful scenes are recorded. Some will scoff at the possibility that such a catastrophe is impending; but perhaps a few will compare the signs of the times with the sure word of prophecy, and escape the coming doom.

Chapter Eleven.

TURKEY AND RUSSIA.

IN order that the prophetic statements concerning Turkey might not be interrupted, some historical facts and opinions of prominent authors and political rulers have been reserved for the present chapter. The reader is asked to notice carefully what is here set forth and also to mark the future development of the Eastern Question along these lines.

For several centuries after the death of Mohammed and his immediate successors, the wild hordes of the desert were under no general government. At last Othman arose, a leader who gathered the scattered factions into some system of order, and from him the name "Ottoman" has been associated with the Turkish Empire. The advent of this warrior is mentioned in Revelation 9,— a chapter generally understood to describe in symbols the progress of this antichristian power. Verse 11 says, "And they had a king over them, which is the angel of the bottomless pit." The destructive character of this government is shown by the names given it,— Abaddon in the Hebrew, and Apollyon in the Greek,—

both words signifying "a destroyer" (see margin). That the Ottoman Empire fully merits such a title, is abundantly proved by past and current history. It seems that its mission is to be a scourge and a destroyer among the nations of the East.

According to Gibbon, Othman and his followers made their first invasion of the Roman Empire in the East, July 27, 1299. The period of their incursions without gaining any substantial victory is given in prophetic language in verse 5. For "five months" they were permitted to "torment" the effete and corrupt civilization of the East, but were restrained from utterly destroying the established empire. In prophecy one day represents a literal year; and so the expression "five months," one hundred and fifty days, represents one hundred and fifty years in literal time. This time ended July 27, 1449, just a hundred and fifty years from the date when Othman entered the empire. During this period, the Turks and Greeks were engaged in almost constant warfare.

After the close of the time indicated in the prophecy, a radical change took place in the success of the Turkish forces, and in 1453 the city of Constantinople fell into their hands, and the Greek division of the Roman Empire was overthrown. From that time to the present, Constantinople has been the capital of the Turkish Empire and the center of the Mohammedan religion. This victorious career is described in the prophecy as follows: —

Loose the four angels which are bound in the great river Euphrates. And the four angels were loosed, which were prepared for an hour, and a day, and a month, and a year, for to slay the third part of men.[1]

By the expression "the third part of men" is meant one of the three divisions into which the Roman Empire was divided. Constantinople was the capital of the eastern portion, and it was this part which became the prey of the Turks.

Notice how definitely the exact time of Turkish supremacy is given — an hour, a day, a month, and a year.

As each day stands for a year, and an hour is the twenty-fourth part of a day, the actual length of time symbolized by this period is 391 years and 15 days. Add this result to July 27, 1449, when the command to "slay" went forth, and we are brought to Aug. 11, 1840. And it is a most remarkable fact that on that very day — Aug. 11, 1840 — Turkish independence virtually ceased, by the sultan's consenting to allow England, Austria, Prussia, and Russia to dictate terms of settlement with the pasha of Egypt, with whom the Porte was then at war.

The ultimatum drawn up by these united powers was first submitted for acceptance to the Turkish government, and by the sultan's agents was placed in the hands of his opposing ruler, on the 11th day of August, 1840. The very day the prophetic period terminated, the Ottoman Empire fell as an inde-

[1] Rev. 9:14, 15.

pendent, self-governing power, and it has ever since existed simply by the toleration of the great powers of Europe. It is a matter of current history and universal knowledge that the control of Turkish affairs rests with the stronger governments of Europe; and the Turk is derisively called the "Sick Man of the East" in recognition of the fact that he is not able to manage his own realm.

We have already referred to the prophecy of Rev. 16 : 12, where the decrease of Turkish resources is symbolized by the drying up of the waters of the Euphrates. This loss has gone on steadily for many years. The following statement, which appeared in the *Public Ledger*, of Philadelphia, of August, 1878, and is quoted in "Daniel and the Revelation," published at Battle Creek, Michigan, expresses very forcibly the gradual shrinking of Turkey's dominion: —

Any one who will take the trouble to look at a map of Turkey in Europe dating back about sixty years, and compare that with the new map sketched by the treaty of San Stefano as modified by the Berlin Congress, will be able to form a judgment of the march of progress that is pressing the Ottoman power out of Europe. Then, the northern boundary of Turkey extended to the Carpathian Mountains, and eastward of the river Sereth it embraced Moldavia as far north nearly as the 47th degree of north latitude. That map embraced also what is now the kingdom of Greece. It covered all of Servia and Bosnia. But by the year 1830 the northern frontier of Turkey was driven back from the Carpathians to the south bank of the Danube, the principalities of Moldavia and Wallachia being emancipated from Turkish domination, and subject only to the payment of an annual tribute in money to the Porte. South of the Danube, the Servians had won a similar emancipation for their country. Greece also had been enabled to establish her independence. Then, as recently, the Turk was truculent and obstinate. Russia and Great Britain proposed to make Greece a tributary state, retaining the sovereignty of the Porte. This was refused, and the result was the utter destruction of the powerful Turkish fleet at Navarino, and the erection of the independent kingdom of Greece. Thus Turkey in Europe was pressed back on all sides. Now, the northern boundary, which was so recently at the Danube, has been driven south to the Balkans. Roumania and Servia have ceased even to be tributary, and have taken their place among independent states. Bosnia has gone under the protection of Austria, as Roumania did under that of Russia in 1829. "Rectified" boundaries give Turkish territory to Servia, Montenegro, and Greece. Bulgaria takes the place of Roumania as a self-governing principality, having no dependence on the Porte, and paying only an annual tribute. Even south of the Balkans the power of the Turk is crippled; for Roumelia is to have "home rule" under a Christian governor. And so again the frontier of Turkey in Europe is pressed back on all sides, until the territory left is but the shadow of what it was sixty years ago. To produce this result has been the policy and the battle of Russia for more than half a century; for nearly that space of time it has been the struggle of some of the other "powers" to maintain the "integrity" of the Turkish Empire. Which policy has succeeded, and which failed, a comparison of maps at intervals of twenty-five years will show. Turkey in Europe has been shriveled up in the last half century. It is shrinking back and back toward Asia, and, though all the "powers" but Russia should unite their forces to maintain the Ottoman system in Europe, there is a manifest destiny visible in the history of the last fifty years that must defeat them.

This writer mentions the policy of Russia, and the anxiety of other nations to thwart these designs. This, in a nutshell, is the Eastern Question as it now stands before the world. Ridpath, in his "Universal History of the World," in speaking of the "Crimean War," thus defines the real issue: —

This conflict began on the Danube in 1853, and received its name from the peninsula of the Crimea, which was the principal theater of the action. The real question at issue was whether Russia might now move to the south, gain control of the Black Sea, overawe the Porte, force her way through the Sea of Marmora into the Archipelago, and thus rectify the mistake of Peter the Great, or whether she should be held back from her manifest destiny, and compelled to limit her commerce to the frozen gulfs of that Eastern Baltic. Such, in a word, was and is that great Eastern Question, the shadow of which has fallen across all the council-tables of Europe for the last thirty years.

The subjugation of Turkey is not merely a recent dream on the part of Russia. It is stated that Peter the Great, who died in 1725, left the following instructions as article 9, in his last will and testament: —

Take every possible means of gaining Constantinople and the Indies (for he who rules there will be the true sovereign of the world); excite war continually in Turkey and Persia; establish fortresses in the Black Sea; get control of the sea by degrees, and also of the Baltic, which is a double point, necessary to the realization of our project; accelerate as much as possible the decay of Persia; penetrate to the Persian Gulf; re-establish, if possible, by the way of Syria, the ancient commerce of the Levant; advance to the Indies, which are the great depot of the world. Once there, we can do without the gold of England.

Steadily and surely Russia is gaining her object, notwithstanding the opposition of other nations, which fear for the stability of their own governments in case Russia secures the advantage she craves. Thus Europe has been a vast checkerboard with empires for men, variously moved hither and thither as the self-interest of the royal players dictated.

From Ridpath's history, before mentioned, we take the following extracts, beginning with events of the year 1828: —

In the same year with the conclusion of peace with Persia, a war was begun by Nicholas with the Turks. The Ottoman power had already entered upon that astonishing decline which has been one of the most striking facts in the history of modern Europe. It was clear, from the first impact of the Russian forces, that the sultan would not be able to make a successful resistance. After a war of only a year's duration, he was glad to purchase peace by ceding to the czar several fortresses on the frontier and along the mouth of the Danube, and by the payment of a large indemnity.

In 1853 the Russian government demanded of the Ottoman Porte certain guaranties of the rights of the Greek Christians of Turkey in Europe. The interference was of a sort to arouse all the fears and suspicions of the sultan, and to excite the hostility of those European powers with which the preservation of the integrity of Turkey had become a cardinal political principle. The sultan regarded the demand of the czar as virtually requiring him to abdicate his sovereignty, and he therefore refused to make the guaranties. In this action he was upheld by England, France, and Sardinia, who became his allies in the struggle which ensued, known as the Crimean War.

After recounting the progress of that war and the defeat of Russia, he enumerates the terms of the treaty limiting the privileges of Russia, and concludes with this sentence: "The integrity of the Ottoman Empire was guaranteed by Great Britain, France, and Austria." Continuing the narrative, he further says: —

In 1860 the Turkish government was rent with a terrible conflict which broke out between the Druses and Maronites, the two religio-political parties of Syria. Several frightful massacres were perpetrated, and a combined squadron of French and English ships was sent to the East in order to put an end to the conflict. In the following year Abdul-Medjid died, and was succeeded by his brother, Abdul-Aziz. . . . The same year witnessed a great insurrection in Crete — an event which led to another war between the Turks and the Greeks. In 1869 a conference of the Western powers was held at Paris, and the difficulties in the Eastern Mediterranean were again adjusted by treaty.

By this time Turkey had become the "Sick Man of the East." The protectorate which had been established over the Ottoman Empire had tended to weaken rather than confirm the grip of the Turk in Europe. A tendency was manifested in all the Turkish provinces to renounce the authority of the Porte and gain their independence. So was it in the Servian insurrection in 1867. So was it with Egypt, which power, after assisting the Turks to put down the Cretan rebellion, sought to throw off the Ottoman rule. A war between Turkey and Egypt was prevented only by the interference of the foreign powers. With the coming of the Franco-Prussian War of 1870–71, the influence of France as one of the protecting states of Turkey was so greatly weakened that Russia, no longer kept in check, was enabled to renew her policy of aggression, and to enforce her will by demanding and obtaining a modification of the treaty of Paris of 1856.

During the decade from 1870 to 1880, the fact became more and more apparent that the Sublime Porte either could not or would not protect the Christians of the Turkish provinces against the bloodthirstiness and oppressions of the Moslems. Outrages and massacres became the order of the day. Now in Bosnia, now in Bulgaria, now in Montenegro, and now in Herzegovina, these scenes of violence and butchery were witnessed, until the sentiment of Christendom was shocked with the repetition. This condition of affairs furnished to Russia her long-coveted excuse for further prosecution of her designs against Turkey. The czar finally made a demand of the six powers which were still pledged to uphold the Ottoman Empire that the outrages perpetrated by the Turks should cease forever, and that the Porte should give a solemn guaranty that they should be no more repeated.

Out of the refusal of the Turkish government to obey the command issued by representatives of the protecting states grew the Turko-Russian War of 1877, which is still fresh in the minds of many who will read these pages. All will remember the short but violent conflict by which Russia pushed her forces almost to the gates of Constantinople, and it appeared for the time that the Ottoman power was about to be crushed. Then it was that the great powers of Europe once more came to the rescue, -

and the Berlin Congress was convened to settle terms for the treaty of peace.

More sanguine persons hoped that at last the Eastern Question was settled; but fresh disturbances continued to alarm the nations at frequent intervals. At last the world was once more aroused by the shocking deeds of violence in Armenia, Constantinople, and Crete during the years 1895–97. The agitation and horror of these recent days has hardly subsided, and the Eastern Question is more alive than ever before.

No candid person can fail to see that the picture drawn by Inspiration is painfully exact. Turkey is indeed a "destroyer," though in justice it should be said that her cruelties have been provoked by intrigues of foreign powers, and rebellion among her own provinces.

No one can fail to see that this power is rapidly being consumed, like the drying up of water beneath a tropical sun ; and this is precisely what the Lord said should come to pass. It will be noticed, too, that his temporary lease of existence is due to the aid of other nations, and that his end will speedily come when such help is withheld. So the Bible declares that *"he shall come to his end, and none shall help him."* [1] This implies that others have previously given him aid, and this we have seen in the course taken by the nations of Europe to save him from Russia's grasp. Already his former friends regret the aid they have rendered, and plainly

[1] Dan. 11 : 45.

declare that henceforth he will be left to his fate, if not even punished by their own hands. A little pamphlet recently published in London, says of England's share in the matter:—

We are responsible for Turkey. We saved the Turk twice at least from the doom which he richly merited. The Duke of Wellington, sixty years ago, lamented that the Russians had not entered Constantinople in 1829, and brought the Ottoman Empire to an end. We have much more reason to lament that it was not destroyed in 1853, and again in 1878. On both these occasions we interfered to save it. But for us, there would be no sultan on the Bosporus.

There is no question that the Turk will soon be left to the covetous clutch of Russia. So the prophecy that "tidings out of the east and out of the *north* shall trouble him," plainly points to Russia as one of the causes of uneasiness. In the very nature of things it cannot be long before Turkey in Europe is no more; and after a brief sojourn in Jerusalem, he comes to an end, as the Bible asserts.[1]

If Turkey were the only nation to suffer when the Eastern Question reaches its culmination, the matter would be serious; but when it is known that all nations will then be involved in a fearful time of trouble, it becomes an appalling crisis to the world. "At that time," continues the prophecy in Dan. 12:1, "there shall be a time of trouble, such as never was since there was a nation." Statesmen

[1] Dan. 11: 44, 45.

of all nations foresee and fear such a result. Lord Salisbury, prime minister of Great Britain, in a speech delivered Nov. 9, 1895, uttered the following words: —

Turkey is in that remarkable condition that it has now stood for half a century, mainly because the great powers of the world have resolved that *for the peace of Christendom it is necessary that the Ottoman Empire should stand.* They came to that conclusion nearly half a century ago. I do not think they have altered it now. The danger, if the Ottoman Empire falls, would not merely be the danger that would threaten the territories of which that empire consists; it would be the danger that the fire there lighted should spread to other nations, and should involve all that are most powerful and civilized in Europe in a dangerous and calamitous contest. That was a danger that was present to the minds of our fathers when they resolved to make the integrity and independence of the Ottoman Empire a matter of European treaty, and *that is a danger which has not passed away.*

The president of Robert College in Constantinople has expressed the following opinion relative to the recent alarm over affairs in the East: —

I believe that there is a general impression among thinking men in Europe that we are approaching a great crisis in the world's history. It is certainly within the bounds of possibility that this year may see the great Christian nations engaged in a universal war.

Such testimony could be multiplied to almost any extent, but it seems unnecessary to say more on this subject; for every thinking person is conscious of a conviction that these are the facts in the case. The question will not be settled by peaceable diplomacy. Discordant elements among the Turk's own subjects will not rest, and cruel measures will surely follow each fresh outbreak. Already the demand is made by the churches and religious bodies that the Turk be driven out; and every outrage will still further inflame the popular hatred of the Christian nations against the infidel followers of Mohammed.

In view of the certain conflict, mighty armies are in readiness. In Bible language we are told that all the kings of the earth and their warriors will be assembled in Palestine, and there will be fought the "battle of that great day of God Almighty."[1]

[1] Rev. 16 : 14.

Chapter Twelve.

THE MODERN CRUSADE.

A NOTEWORTHY sign of the times is found in the widespread belief that a future age of glorious gospel triumphs is about to be ushered in. This idea constitutes an important part in the belief of nearly all religious people, and to doubt or deny its claim is considered heresy, if not infidelity. The "one undying enthusiasm" of all who entertain this view is to "make Christ this world's king." To this end they bend every energy.

When one error is embraced, it leads to another, and these with increased force demand a third, and so on in ever-increasing ratio, until the whole truth is perverted. The first falsehood cannot stand alone undetected; hence a second is added to cover the first, and a tissue is rapidly woven that partially conceals the inherent weakness of the whole; and, being long-cherished, these theories pass as actual truth, and the true view is denounced as false.

In the subjects under consideration in this book, we see this principle illustrated. When the incorrect doctrine that Christ is to reign in this present world has been imbibed, the next logical step in error is the world's conversion. This, too, is entirely contrary to the plain teaching of the Bible; but it necessarily accompanies the other, for no one can suppose that Christ will reign over men in their sinful state. But experience shows that men are slow to choose the right way under conditions now prevalent; therefore the theory of a better future age is devised to uphold these two falsehoods. The fourth step in this compound error is, that in the future age evil will be so removed from the reach of men by the binding of Satan that nothing but conversion will be left for them. The fifth step is to try to secure laws in the "Christian nations" by which the unconverted will have no option in the matter, but their religion will be regulated by statutes from Parliament or Congress. The sixth and last deception, designed to make the others appear plausible, is to consider almost any outward profession, and acceptance of church forms, even when enforced by the civil laws, as genuine conversion.

Thus, to reverse the order; a superficial "form of godliness" now passes for Christianity. Persons who give no Bible evidence of knowing the power of God in their lives, are retained and considered respectable members of the church, and at death they are lauded as eminent examples of piety. Out of such material, "Christian nations" are made. War, drunkenness, political intrigue, and various wicked practises are covered over by the words "patriotism," "public revenue," "diplomacy," "statesmanship," "public spirit," etc. Then these same nations pose as God's messengers to convert the "heathen." The unconverted at home are to be reached by national laws which will make it a crime to disregard the forms of religion; and the heathen abroad are to be taught by armed force to respect the gospel. Thus the world will be converted, and Christ will come and reign on David's throne.

This is no fancy picture. Any one who will look carefully will see that, however honest the actors may be, and however unconscious of what they are doing, this is the tendency in much that passes for religious faith and activity. And the case is worse when some of these same nations are "identified" as "lost Israel," who are to receive all the blessings promised to the saints and martyrs of God in the world to come. The head aches and the heart is faint when the situation is comprehended. God accepts nothing but a loving service. He does not shut up the people nor bind Satan, in order to compel men who love sin to pretend to be religious; every one is left free to choose his own master. God has not asked the church to convert the world, but to preach the gospel to all, though he has told us that only a few will enter the strait and narrow way that leads to life. And he has assured us that, in due time, he will bestow the kingdom on the Son, without any aid from the nations of earth.

What has all this to do with the Eastern Question?— Much every way; chiefly because this modern crusade will yet be turned especially toward Turkey in expectation of preparing the way for Christ to come to Jerusalem, and begin a reign of peace over the whole earth. Gradually the mass of unscriptural teaching which clusters around the Eastern Question is exposed. We have already seen that the dominion of the Turk is to be dried up, and that at last he will come to his end with none to help him. In connection with this, we have also learned that the battle of the great day of God Almighty will be waged, and that a time of trouble of unparalleled extent and severity will then come upon the nations. It is evident that some strong religious excitement will lead the nations to that fatal spot; for John thus describes the hidden agency in the movement: —

And I saw three unclean spirits like frogs. . . . They are the spirits of devils, working miracles, which go forth unto the kings of the earth and of the whole world, to gather them to the battle of that great day of God Almighty.[1]

From this we learn that Satan and his host are the unseen leaders of the armies of the nations. But he will disguise the nature of his work, and make it appear as a warfare for Christ and the gospel. His power in this respect is described by the apostle Paul: —

[1] Rev. 16: 13, 14.

For such are false apostles, deceitful workers, transforming themselves into the apostles of Christ. And no marvel; for Satan himself is transformed into an angel of light. Therefore it is no great thing if his ministers also be transformed as the ministers of righteousness; whose end shall be according to their works.[1]

No one who regards the authority of the Scriptures can fail to see that Satan will lead the blinded nations to the Holy Land. In the most specious manner he will influence his human agents to urge forward the grand crusade. They will press the matter upon the rulers and people as something demanded by humanity and by Christianity. In short, the nations will be urged to combine for the purpose of suppressing Turkish misrule and settling the Eastern Question. The prophecy distinctly teaches that any expedition of this kind will be under the strongest religious enthusiasm.

And now we ask the reader to look over recent events, and see if he can discern any agitation tending in this direction. Have we not seen the churches, chapels, and clergy almost in a frenzy of unrest over the Turkish atrocities in Armenia, Crete, Constantinople, and other places in the sultan's territory? Have not mass-meetings, conventions, and conferences signified the general desire for the Turks to be "blotted out," even though war should be necessary? Has it not been claimed that such a conflict would be a "holy war"? Has it not been demanded in the name of God, and in

[1] 2 Cor. 11:13-15.

the interests of "humanity" and "Christianity"? Has it not been asserted that the wrath of God would be visited on the "Christian nations" which would not act in this crisis? In short, have we not already witnessed the beginning of a crusade to the East in which religious enthusiasm is the leading factor? These things have not been done in a corner; all nations are involved. Who can say that some supernatural agency is not instigating the Turk to commit the atrocities that lead to this unusual excitement?

It is true that civil rulers have been slow to move, and thus far the issue is avoided. Leading statesmen have expressed their fears that a move would precipitate a general war. They dare not rush into the breach. The subject is full of dire possibilities. We need not suppose the matter is permanently settled, even though comparative peace may ensue for an interval. Satan has not yet exhausted his deceptions. He will stir up the fanatical Turks to further massacres, and the infuriated provinces to further resistance. Thus minds will be inflamed to execute vengeance on the infidel followers of a false religion.

The prophecy declares that "miracles" will be wrought by these evil spirits, still further to inflame the world. Christ has given the warning, that great signs and wonders will be performed of a kind to deceive all but the elect. The magicians of Egypt did miracles before Pharaoh, which led to the ruin of his proud army; and the frog-like power that performs these modern miracles, peeping and muttering its pretended revelations from the dead, is of the same character. Already a wonder-working religion has appeared in Spiritualism, Theosophy, and kindred occult forces. Grant for a moment that Satan is able to work miracles through these channels, and what is to hinder the development of supernatural forces far beyond what we now know to exist? The Bible declares both the cause and the effect to be certain. In Revelation we read:—

> And he doeth great wonders, so that he maketh fire come down from heaven on the earth in the sight of men, and deceiveth them that dwell on the earth.[1]

We need not speculate as to the precise manner in which the deception will come; but the fact that the world will be deceived, and that under this false influence the armies of the nations will gather in the East for a final struggle, is as certain as that the Bible is true. Another remarkable fact is that the nations are arming for this very conflict. What keeps the powers of Europe in suspense?—The Eastern Question. They instinctively feel that a crash is coming. And it will come.

In the midst of all this preparation for war, another astounding fact appears. Nearly everybody is expecting an era of perfect peace. Men dream of a good time coming, when war will be no more. Indeed, they hope that when the Eastern Question

[1] Rev. 13:13, 14.

is settled, the millennium can begin. Some reckless ones assert that the millennium has already begun, and that the best guaranty of peace is that the military powers are now so strong that none will dare to provoke a fight. Others expect a terrible war will result from the present strained relations of each government in the race; but when this is once over, they look for permanent peace. According to this view, the way to have peace is to fight; the way to bring in the millennium is to have a general war. Then the Lord can establish his kingdom at Jerusalem, bind Satan, and fulfil the dreams of a future age.

SWORDS AND PLOWSHARES.

Popular ideas are illustrated by the following prophecy : —

And it shall come to pass in the last days, that the mountain of the Lord's house shall be established in the top of the mountains, and shall be exalted above the hills; and all nations shall flow unto it. And many people shall go and say, Come ye, and let us go up to the mountain of the Lord, to the house of the God of Jacob; and he will teach us of his ways, and we will walk in his paths; for out of Zion shall go forth the law, and the word of the Lord from Jerusalem. And he shall judge among the nations, and shall rebuke many people; and they shall beat their swords into plowshares, and their spears into pruning-hooks: nation shall not lift up sword against nation, neither shall they learn war any more.[1]

[1] Isa. 62 : 2-4.

Probably all have heard these words often repeated, and applied to the "good time" expected during the "millennium." Let us therefore carefully examine them. Notice, first, that these things are to be spoken in the "*last days.*" They are now heard on every side; hence we may know that we have reached that time. "Mountains," when taken figuratively, denote support, defense, and strength. The "Lord's house" must be the church. The language used indicates that the church here described receives her support, defense, and strength from the governments of earth. This aid may be secured by general laws on religious doctrines in harmony with popular belief, as well as by one particular denomination receiving official recognition from the state. When Christian people look to Parliament, Congress, or any earthly authority to support the gospel, they put their trust in men instead of God. The governments of earth are their defense and support, and the nominal church is "exalted above the hills." Religious forms become popular under the sanction and support of civil authority, and the result is just what the prophecy asserts,— "All nations shall flow unto it."

It is needless to say that the spirit of apostasy is already at work in any church before she will turn to national help, and solicit governmental patronage; and when an illicit union is once formed between the church and the state, both are still further corrupted. This was the policy of the Roman

Church,—the "mother of harlots,"—and, alas! her Protestant daughters have followed her example until there are "established" churches in nearly all the nations, and those not honored with a connection with the government are becoming infected with the idea that civil laws must be framed to protect the interests of religion, and so hasten the reign of Christ. Under the influence of this "wine of Babylon," the difference between the true church in obscurity and the brazen harlot in public places is not noticed, except to jeer the modest one because of her prudish ways.

Especial attention is invited to the source from which the call to go up to Jerusalem emanates. "*Many people* shall go and say" this. In this case the voice of the people is not the voice of God. He is not the one who calls the nations to this movement. And do we not now hear "many people" expressing these thoughts?—Yes, and in the very words of this prophecy. Their one "vital, organic thought" is to win this world for Christ, and crown him king. To this end they ask that the church shall be supported by the state, so that the strong arm of the law may cause the people to *flow* (down grade, of course) into the church. The leaders on every side are ready for the flow to begin, and many openly advocate these measures.

Next observe the locality where their hopes center. "Out of *Zion* shall go forth the law, and the word of the Lord from *Jerusalem.*" Remember that is what "many people" say. Jerusalem is the spot whence the law of the Lord will go forth, and of course the Turk must be driven out. No doubt many at present attach a figurative meaning to the terms, but others expect the prophecy to be literally fulfilled; and under the deceptions yet to come, there is no doubt but that all will eventually look for the personal reign of Christ to begin in Jerusalem.

Please observe again what "many people" say about further war after they meet at Jerusalem: —

And he shall judge among the nations, and shall rebuke many people; and they shall beat their swords into plowshares, and their spears into pruning-hooks: nation shall not lift up sword against nation, neither shall they learn war any more.

Are not these very words quoted to prove that a good time is coming? Well, the Lord said that "*many people*" would say this, and they are saying it; but, alas! many think the *Lord* has said it. Reader, can you discern the difference between the words of God and those of "many people"? We will see; please study another scripture: —

Proclaim ye this among the Gentiles: Prepare war, wake up the mighty men, let all the men of war draw near; let them come up. Beat your plowshares into swords, and your pruning-hooks into spears: let the weak say, I am strong. Assemble yourselves, and come, all ye heathen, and gather yourselves together round about: thither cause thy mighty ones to come down, O Lord. Let the heathen be wakened, and come up to the valley of Jehoshaphat: for there will I sit to judge all the heathen round about. Put ye in the sickle, for the harvest is ripe: come, get you down; for the press is full, the fats overflow; for their wickedness is great. Multitudes, multitudes in the valley of decision: for the day of the Lord is near in the valley of decision. The sun and the moon shall be darkened, and the stars shall withdraw their shining. The Lord also shall roar out of Zion, and utter his voice from Jerusalem; and the heavens and the earth shall shake: but the Lord will be the hope of his people, and the strength of the children of Israel. So shall ye know that I am the Lord your God dwelling in Zion, my holy mountain: then shall Jerusalem be holy, and there shall no stranger pass through her any more.[1]

In the foregoing words we have the Lord's prediction of what *will* take place at the very time when "many people" *say* something else is coming. No one can doubt that they are intended to show opposite sides of the same picture. The language is similar, but the thought is reversed. They both describe the same period of time; in one it is called the "last days;" in the other it is said, "The day of the Lord is near." Both refer to the same locality. Jerusalem and Mount Zion are mentioned in one, and the valley of Jehoshaphat, near the city, in the other. Both treat upon the same subject. And yet in all essential particulars, one is the exact opposite of the other. "Many people" do not agree with the Lord about this matter.

We have commented in detail upon their statements; now let us note what God says. He says

[1] Joel 3: 9-17.

there will be war — not that he desires it to be so, but because it is what the nations trust in for protection. "Many people" say they "will learn war no more;" but the Lord says, "Wake up the mighty men, let all the men of war draw near." They say, "Beat your swords into plowshares;" he says, "Beat your plowshares into swords." Let men of reason say which of these predictions is finding its fulfilment, — the words of many people, or the words of God. *Are* the nations beating their swords into plowshares, or are they doing just the contrary? *Are* they disarming their troops, or are they levying more? Have they closed any military schools, dismantled any forts, sold any gunboats? God says they will prepare war. Are they doing so? The earth trembles with the march of armed men. The waters foam with the powerful navies. The shops groan with the preparation of implements of destruction.

Who are engaging in the rush for blood? — The "Christian nations," the "people." What is it all for? — The Eastern Question. Where will they meet? — At Jerusalem, in the valley of Jehoshaphat. What is the result? — "Multitudes, multitudes, in the valley of *concision,* or, *threshing,*" margin. There the nations are cut off. "Their wickedness is great, the press is *full.*" Here is the "fulness of the Gentiles." Beneath the same city walls where the ancient Jews drank from the cup of wrath they had filled to the brim, the Gentiles will receive the judgment due to their "fulness" of iniquity. Instead of Jerusalem being the "city of peace," it will be the hell of war.

False views of the kingdom of God and the reign of the Messiah on David's throne, caused national Israel to become exalted in their blindness, until the city of their pride, over which Jesus wept in compassion, became their sepulcher. In a similar manner, the modern nations have lost sight of the true people of God and the true nature of the promises, until they too are looking for the kingdom to be set up at Jerusalem, with themselves the favored ones. Over and over does the Lord in pity warn them of the coming doom, and weep over their blindness. Nothing but destruction — a tomb without a burial — awaits those who are led to Jerusalem by the agents of Satan.

Woe to the multitude of many people, which make a noise like the noise of the seas; and to the rushing of nations, that make a rushing like the rushing of mighty waters! The nations shall rush like the rushing of many waters; but God shall rebuke them, and they shall flee far off, and shall be chased as the chaff of the mountains before the wind, and like a rolling thing before the whirlwind. And behold at eveningtide trouble; and before the morning he is not. This is the portion of them that spoil us, and the lot of them that rob us.[1]

O ye children of Benjamin, gather yourselves to flee out of the midst of Jerusalem; . . . for evil appeareth out of the north, and great destruction.[2]

[1] Isa. 17: 12–14.   [2] Jer. 6: 1.

Reader, both sides of the question are partially before you. God is seeking to lead his people away from the strife of earth ; but Satan is bending every energy to involve the nations in war. In this chapter we have compared four separate prophecies which treat directly on the culmination of the Eastern Question in Palestine. They agree in ascribing a time of trouble to all the nations. By taking heed to the truth, we may be spared that calamity.

Chapter Thirteen.

THE DAY OF THE LORD.

IN the Scriptures, frequent use is made of the expression, "the day of the Lord;" and as this day is directly connected with the Eastern Question, a chapter will be devoted to its consideration. Since much of the value of this argument depends upon the harmony in all its parts, we must be pardoned for frequent repetition of some particulars. But as the evidences multiply with each new topic, the reader is asked to carry in mind the previous deductions, and apply them at each advance step. If any point does not seem perfectly plain at first, please study the chapter devoted to this special subject, which will be easily found by the index, and then reread the difficult passage. After we have settled a principle, it must be applied in further study. The mathematician remembers that two and two make four in cube root as well as in simple addition. In the same way we must study first principles in divine truth until they are used almost involuntarily in the deep things of God.

No one has a right to attach an arbitrary meaning to the Scriptures, simply to build up a theory. Each portion, when rightly understood, will not only be clear and consistent in itself, but it will be in perfect harmony with the remainder of the Scriptures. It is difficult for error to appear perfectly consistent in even one passage; it is much more difficult to make it seem in accord with several different passages; and it is impossible for it to be so adjusted as to agree with the entire Bible.

The themes presented in this book are much discussed, with widely divergent views, which are no doubt quite unintelligible to the ordinary Bible reader. Much discredit has thus been cast upon these subjects by those who care little for prophetic study, and much confusion exists among those who profess an interest in these things. Our object is to examine each statement solely on its own merits, then to compare conclusions from these various sources, and so step by step to confirm our position. No theory is adopted simply because it may be popular; none is discarded because it may be unpopular. We are anxious for truth alone. Acting on this principle, we have found that "Israel" is a title expressive of a righteous character, which can only be obtained through faith in Christ, and conformity to the law of God. This definition is repeatedly emphasized by Christ and the apostles. No one should hesitate so to understand this word, except where it is plainly used in a secondary sense to denote the whole or part of the Hebrew nation.

In accordance with this first conclusion, we next learn that the promised inheritance for Israel is in a world yet to be created; now the people of God are pilgrims and strangers, looking for that "better country." They also have a city, the New Jerusalem, now above, in heaven, but which is to come down and remain upon the new earth.

A third conclusion is that Christ will not reign over this present world, but in the world to come. This present earth will pass away in a flood of fire, even as the former earth perished in a flood of water. Preparatory to such a change, and before Christ takes the throne of David, he must finish his work as priest on the Father's throne; and this work, we are assured, is now going forward in the "cleansing" of the sanctuary, so that the sins of redeemed Israel may be put on Satan, the scapegoat, before his destruction.

Another logical and Scriptural conclusion follows from these facts; namely, probation for the race, or the work of the gospel, will soon be finished; and after that work is done, the world's conversion, either in the present or a future age, is a fable. On all these points the Bible testimony is conclusive, and each one is the natural sequence of the preceding deductions. Thus the direct argument is fortified at every step by new evidence.

Turning now to the negative side, we find each link strongly forged and interlocked with its neighbors, forming a chain which cannot be broken, a cable of infinite strength. Indeed, we find that no promises are made to men by natural birth, whether

Jew or Gentile; consequently there will be no gathering of these nations by the Lord. On the contrary, we learn that Satan will deceive the world on this matter, and cause the nations to assemble in Palestine for the battle of the great day of God. In connection with this event, many religious teachers are predicting a glorious reign of Christ to begin at Jerusalem, and "many people" are turning their eyes thither, and placing their hopes on that event. Also the nations and kings of the earth are preparing their armies with the express purpose of being ready for a crisis which is evidently near. Turkey, as indicated in the prophecy, is to be "dried up" to open the way for a rush to the Holy Land. Thus the Eastern Question is already asking the world, Are you ready? And there and then will come upon the deceived people, church and state, the "fulness of the Gentiles," the "time of trouble," the battle of "Armageddon," the dashing in "pieces like a potter's vessel," the "end of the world." With this review, let us proceed to further testimony concerning the "day of the Lord," or the "great day," as it is frequently called.

Probably no one will claim that the day of the Lord is an ordinary day of twenty-four hours. All understand that it is a period of time, in the same way that the present age is called the "day of salvation," the "day of grace," etc. Our first point is to ascertain when it will begin. No definite date is given in the Scriptures; but we can judge approximately of its approach by observing the signs of the times, and the events with which it is connected. We have already found that the battle of Armageddon will be in "the great day of God Almighty;" and as this occurs in connection with the drying up of the river Euphrates, or the destruction of the Turkish Empire, we can judge of its proximity; for from indications everywhere apparent, the end of Turkey is near.

The prophecy of Joel, which has already been considered, points to the preparations for war now seen on all sides, and says that the "day of the Lord is near." In short, the Eastern Question is the preparation the world is making for the day of the Lord, and the battle of the great day of God. Again, we have learned from the prophecy in Isa. 2:2-4 that in the "last days" "many people" will be expecting a time of universal peace to begin at Jerusalem. This theory is now held in some form by nearly all religious bodies.

Finally, we have learned that Christ is finishing his work of grace as our priest at the right hand of God. From all these different lines of evidence, we learn that the "day of salvation" is soon to close, and that the day of the Lord is near. Many other signs might be mentioned teaching the same truth; but as they are not so directly connected with the general subject, these will suffice. The reader can readily see their solemn import. All should be carefully studied.

LIKE A THIEF IN THE NIGHT.

We are assured that the "day of the Lord so cometh as a thief in the night." This will be readily understood when it is remembered that the termination of Christ's ministry as priest in heaven will mark the close of the day of salvation and the beginning of the day of the Lord. Those who ignore the truth concerning the cleansing of the heavenly sanctuary, where his final work of atonement is performed, will know nothing about the approaching end, and while they are fondly hoping for a future age of greater gospel light, the only gospel ever offered to man will be withdrawn. On the other hand, those who by faith follow their priest into the second apartment of the sanctuary — even as in the "pattern" on earth, by the sound of the tinkling bells on the garments of the high priest — will know what is about to take place. Both these classes are mentioned in contrast concerning the day of the Lord, as follows: —

> But of the times and the seasons, brethren, ye have no need that I write unto you. For yourselves know perfectly that the day of the Lord so cometh as a thief in the night. For when they shall say, Peace and safety; then sudden destruction cometh upon them, as travail upon a woman with child; and they shall not escape. But ye, brethren, are not in darkness, that that day should overtake you as a thief.[1]

Notice this quotation carefully. One class will be saying, "Peace and safety" at the very time

[1] 1 Thess. 5: 1-4.

when the day of the Lord is at hand. They have not believed that the work of Christ is to close in the heavenly sanctuary; but they have expected him to come to this earth, be crowned king at Jerusalem, usher in an era of peace, and convert the world. O fatal delusion! While their eyes are turned toward a future age, the opportunity of the present hour is lost. While they sleep in supposed security, dreaming of a glorious millennium, the day of mercy closes forever, and the day of the Lord is ushered in.

The other class have not been deceived; they have known the truth. They do not cry, "Peace and safety;" but they fulfil the word of the Lord through his prophet: "Blow ye the trumpet in Zion, and sound an alarm in my holy mountain; let all the inhabitants of the land tremble: for the day of the Lord cometh, for it is nigh at hand."[1] They have pointed men to the only refuge in the coming storm. They are Paul's "brethren" in the last days, true Israelites, children of the light. The day of the Lord does not come upon them like a thief. They do not know the day nor the hour when the work in heaven will be done; but their names have been confessed before the Father and the angels, and stand recorded in the Lamb's book of life. Both these classes are in the world to-day. Reader, with which will you stand?

[1] Joel 2 : 1.

A DAY OF DARKNESS.

Possibly some who admit that the day of the Lord is near, may still think that it will not bring the close of probation to all the wicked, but that instead it will be a glad day to many on this earth. For the benefit of such we quote a few texts: —

Woe unto you that desire the day of the Lord! to what end is it for you? the day of the Lord is darkness, and not light. As if a man did flee from a lion, and a bear met him; or went into the house, and leaned his hand on the wall, and a serpent bit him. Shall not the day of the Lord be darkness, and not light? even very dark, and no brightness in it.[1]

For the day of the Lord cometh, for it is nigh at hand; a day of darkness and of gloominess; . . . there hath not been ever the like, neither shall be any more after it, even to the years of many generations.[2]

Howl ye; for the day of the Lord is at hand; it shall come as a destruction from the Almighty. . . . Behold, the day of the Lord cometh, cruel both with wrath and fierce anger, to lay the land desolate; and he shall destroy the sinners thereof out of it.[3]

This is the uniform teaching of the Bible.

THE FINAL DECREE.

Attention has been called to the fact that probation will close when the time is reached for Christ to take the throne of David. From the very nature of the case, this must be true; for there is no priesthood, and consequently can be no atonement,

---

[1] Amos 5:18-20.   [2] Joel 2:1, 2.   [3] Isa. 13:6-9.

after Christ assumes the government in his kingdom; but we have a direct statement that the destiny of all men is decided before Christ comes to this earth: —

He that is unjust, let him be unjust still: and he which is filthy, let him be filthy still: and he that is righteous, let him be righteous still: and he that is holy, let him be holy still. And, behold, I come quickly; and my reward is with me, to give every man according as his work shall be.[1]

Notice that this decree is made *before* Christ appears, or, as already learned, when his work in the true sanctuary is done, and while the world will be unaware of what is taking place in heaven. Notice, too, that every man's condition has been forever settled when that moment comes; the unrighteous cannot then be made righteous, and the holy will not become unholy. Hence there will be no further preaching of the gospel, and no more conversions to the Lord after that time. In short, it is the day of God's vengeance, preparatory to the passing away of this world, to be succeeded by the world to come.

THE SEVEN LAST PLAGUES.

In addition to a general description of the day of wrath, the Bible mentions "seven last plagues," with the statement that, "in them is filled up the wrath of God."[2] These will be the dregs of that awful cup yet to be wrung out to the nations which forget God. Again it is spoken of emphatically as

[1] Rev. 22 : 11, 12.   [2] Rev. 15 : 1.

the "wine of the wrath of God, which is poured out without mixture into the cup of his indignation."[1] Until probation closes, the wrath of God is mixed with mercy, but the end of Christ's ministration on the Father's throne will seal the sinner's doom. Then the cup of a long-suffering God will be "full," and the "fulness of the Gentiles" will have "come in."

By no possible stretch of reason or Scripture can these plagues be assigned to a past age. Language and logic both place them in the future, after the day of the Lord begins. They will constitute the "time of trouble," noticed in Dan. 12:1, which is to take place when the Turk comes to his end, and Michael, or Christ, stands up. In some respects they appear to have been foreshadowed by the plagues sent upon Pharaoh and the Egyptians when the Lord delivered his people Israel. When the seven last plagues are poured out, the true Israel will be delivered.

In Revelation 16, each plague is separately mentioned. The first six are somewhat local, but the last is universal. Under the sixth plague the Turkish Empire will come to an end, as stated in verse 12. In connection with that event, the spirits of devils lead the nations to Armageddon, to the battle of the great day. Then the last plague falls, and the voice of God declares, "It is done."

Christ has said that the days just before his appearing will be like those in the time of Noah

---

[1] Rev. 14:10.

before the flood. The antediluvian day of probation ended when God shut Noah in the ark, and all the wicked were shut out; but it was seven days before the flood came. In their cases, all hope was gone; yet they continued to plant and build, eat and drink, marry and give in marriage, "and knew not until the flood came, and took them all away; so shall also the coming of the Son of Man be."[1] Hence we may conclude that even after the close of probation to all the world, the wicked will go on in their accustomed business and pleasure, unconscious of their true condition, until the last plague, that of great hail, shall burst upon them, and they find themselves without shelter, while vainly calling for rocks and mountains to cover them from the face of him that sitteth on the throne.

RIGHTEOUS ISRAEL DELIVERED.

Another point deserves notice. While the plagues fall upon the wicked, the people of God will be protected. This was the case with Noah and his family during the flood, with Lot and his daughters at the destruction of Sodom, with the Hebrews during the plagues of Egypt, and with the disciples at the destruction of old Jerusalem. So from analogy we might be sure that true Israel will escape all that comes upon the world in its final dissolution. This supposition is made sure by the words of the psalmist: —

[1] Matt. 24 : 38, 39.

He that dwelleth in the secret place of the Most High shall abide under the shadow of the Almighty. . . . Surely he shall deliver thee from the snare of the fowler, and from the noisome pestilence. He shall cover thee with his feathers, and under his wings shalt thou trust: his truth shall be thy shield and buckler. Thou shalt not be afraid for the terror by night; nor for the arrow that flieth by day; nor for the pestilence that walketh in darkness; nor for the destruction that wasteth at noonday. A thousand shall fall at thy side, and ten thousand at thy right hand; but it shall not come nigh thee. Only with thine eyes shalt thou behold and see the reward of the wicked. Because thou hast made the Lord, which is my refuge, even the Most High, thy habitation; there shall no evil befall thee, neither shall any plague come nigh thy dwelling.[1]

Now we can understand another scripture which has been strangely distorted, namely, the gathering of the eagles to the carcass. First we will quote a few verses: —

I tell you, in that night there shall be two men in one bed; the one shall be taken [Greek, "seized"], and the other shall be left [Greek, "escape"]. Two women shall be grinding together; the one shall be taken, and the other left. Two men shall be in the field; the one shall be taken, and the other left. And they answered and said unto him, Where, Lord? And he said unto them, Wheresoever the body is, thither will the eagles be gathered together.[2]

In Matt. 24:28 the word "carcass" is used instead of "body." Many suppose those "taken" are the righteous, who are caught up to meet Christ in the air, while those "left" are the unsaved; but it must be apparent that such a view makes Christ

[1] Ps. 91:1-10.   [2] Luke 17:34-37.

the "carcass," and the saints the "eagles"! Our sense of propriety is shocked by the thought of comparing the living Saviour to a dead body, a putrid carcass, and the saints, who are commanded to be as "harmless as doves," to ravenous, filthy "eagles"! This incongruous application vanishes, when it is seen that those who are "taken" are the wicked, who are indeed a dead body, a carcass, to be seized by the "seven last plagues," as represented by the "eagles" feasting on the slain; and those who are "left" are the righteous Israel, on whom the plagues have no power; for they are safe under the wings of the Almighty. His truth is their shield and buckler.

THE COMING OF CHRIST.

The second coming of Christ must not be confounded with the coming of the day of the Lord. The two events are entirely different in many respects. His coming takes place *in* the day of the Lord, but it is not itself the day of the Lord. This distinction is clearly marked by the following points of contrast: —

1. The "day of the Lord" begins immediately after the close of the "day of salvation," or at the time when Christ leaves the Father's throne to take his own throne of David; following this change is the infliction of the seven last plagues, which must occupy a brief period of time. But the coming of Christ takes place after the plagues have fallen;

for in Rev. 16 : 15 his coming is shown to be still in the future after the first six plagues have been poured out. Therefore, in point of *time* the opening of the day of the Lord precedes the coming of the Lord by a short interval.

2. The day of the Lord comes like a thief in the night, silently, unseen, and unexpectedly, while men are buying, selling, planting, and building. But the coming of Christ will be like the "lightning coming out of the east, and shining even unto the west;" a glorious coming with "all the holy angels as attendants;" a descent from heaven "with a shout, with the voice of the archangel, and with the trump of God;" an appearing in which "every eye shall see him;" a personal, literal, visible coming in the same manner as he went away, not a coming in the "desert" or the "secret chamber;" a coming when the wicked will know of his appearing, and flee from his presence, with calls to the rocks and mountains to cover them. Certainly here are differences that cannot be overlooked. It is impossible to apply all these expressions to the same event. No thief comes shouting, blowing a trumpet, and lighting up the entire place where his robbery is to be committed. Therefore, in point of *manner*, the day of the Lord is not the same as the coming of Christ.

By mixing things so diverse in their nature, men have invented dangerous theories. They talk about a secret coming of the Lord, unknown to the world generally, at which a few will be caught up to meet the Lord in the air. This they call the "eagles" gathering to the "carcass," etc. It is not necessary to mention more of the absurd inferences handed out for "new light." No one can avoid such errors unless he knows that the day of the Lord begins at the close of Christ's ministry in the true sanctuary, unmarked by any special event on earth; and that Christ's coming is a visible, glorious appearing after the time of trouble, after the battle of the great day of God Almighty, after the dashing in pieces of the nations, and after the pouring out of the wine of the wrath of God in the seven last plagues. By marking these contrasts, we may avoid wrong conclusions, give to each text its proper meaning, and learn the truth, which will be our shield in that awful day when the wrath of the Lamb shall come. Indifference will be fatal to as many as cherish it; for those who do not receive the love of the truth will be left to believe a lie; and they will find, when too late, that the harvest is past, the summer is ended, and they are not saved.

Other remarks concerning the duration and end of the day of the Lord will be reserved to a following chapter, after we have sketched more fully the position and work of the true Israel of God in these closing days. At this point our comment on the Eastern Question may be expressed in the words of the prophet: —

Watchman, what of the night? Watchman, what of the night? The watchman said, The morning cometh, and also the night; if ye will inquire, inquire ye: *return, come.*[1]

Morning breaks for Israel, but with it night comes to the Gentiles. Which shall it be to us?

[1] Isa. 21:11, 12.

Chapter Fourteen.

THE FOUR WINDS.

OUR way is now cleared to another very interesting prophecy connected with Israel and the Eastern Question, a portion of which we quote:—

And after these things I saw four angels standing on the four corners of the earth, holding the four winds of the earth, that the wind should not blow on the earth, nor on the sea, nor on any tree. And I saw another angel ascending from the east, having the seal of the living God: and he cried with a loud voice to the four angels, to whom it was given to hurt the earth and the sea, saying, Hurt not the earth, neither the sea, nor the trees, till we have sealed the servants of our God in their foreheads. And I heard the number of them which were sealed: and there were sealed an hundred and forty and four thousand of all the tribes of the children of Israel.[1]

Attention is first directed to the time when this sealing work will be done. John says, "And after these things." To what things did he refer? Going back to the closing part of the preceding chapter, we have a record of the events which occur under the sixth seal. A glance at them shows that they all pertain to the closing days of this world's history. We quote:—

[1] Rev. 7:1-4.

And the heaven departed as a scroll when it is rolled together; and every mountain and island were moved out of their places. And the kings of the earth, and the great men, and the rich men, and the chief captains, and the mighty men, and every bondman, and every freeman, hid themselves in the dens and in the rocks of the mountains; and said to the mountains and rocks, Fall on us, and hide us from the face of Him that sitteth on the throne, and from the wrath of the Lamb; for the great day of his wrath is come; and who shall be able to stand?[1]

Most of the scenes here described have been made familiar in the study of other prophecies. Once more the great gathering of the kings of the earth and their chief captains and mighty men is described on the sacred page. It is the Eastern Question over again, the same company Joel saw in the valley of Jehoshaphat, that Daniel saw in the time of trouble, and John at the place called Armageddon. While thus assembled, every cheek turns pale. Great hailstones, which God has "reserved against the time of trouble, against the day of battle and war,"[2] will then be poured out of the armory of heaven, "every stone about the weight of a talent"[3] — at least sixty pounds. What cannon can reply to such missiles from the fort of heaven? What gunboat can be trained on the unseen power? What can man do contending with God? Then the proud warriors realize their weakness, and vainly beseech the mountains to hide them from that face soon to be seen coming in the clouds of heaven.

[1] Rev. 6:14-17.   [2] Job 38:23.   [3] Rev. 16:21.

After beholding this scene, John turns to another view, in which the people of God pass before his eyes. God has not forgotten Israel in the days of peril. The prophet sees four angels holding the four winds, evidently about to let them blow; but another angel bids them hold until the servants of God are sealed — twelve thousand out of each tribe of true Israel.

SYMBOLS EXPLAINED.

What is meant by the *four winds?* — Evidently they are the symbol of war and strife; for they are used in relation to the battle array of the kings of the earth. The same thing is represented by them in the vision of Dan. 7:2: "The four winds of the heaven strove upon the great sea. And four great beasts came up from the sea." These beasts are said to be "four kings [kingdoms], which shall arise out of the earth." Nations rise and fall by war and conquest; and the four winds, lashing the sea to fury, must denote the wars by which these different powers were brought successively into prominence. We are informed that "sea," or "waters," represents people.[1] How striking are these figures — "sea" means people; "winds," war; "beasts," the nations which come up.

Turning again to Rev. 7:1, we understand from the terms used that preparations for war are rapidly going forward, and that at times it looks as if a general struggle must come; and then the moaning

[1] Rev. 17:15.

winds die away in their dark recesses, only to sweep back again with a stronger gust, impatient for the restraint to be removed that they may break out for the whirlwind's work of death.

Such is the picture of the outcome of the Eastern Question which Inspiration has painted before us. The world has gazed at it for many years, wondering what it means. The nations are straining at their chains, eager to resent the least insult to their dignity, to revenge old grudges, or to acquire new possessions. Is not this the present situation all over the world? Has it not been the history of the present generation? How often the news has flashed along the telegraph wires that at last the spark to start the conflagration has been kindled! The press has discussed the situation pro and con; the scattered fleets have been gathered in; talk of war has been heard on every side; "bulls and bears" have contended on the stock exchanges over the prospects of strife: and then the scare has subsided; the atmosphere has become clear again, and men have laughed at the idea of any real danger. In a few months the play is acted over again, with the same result. This has been the experience of the last quarter of a century. Over and over, and over again, the surging tide has been driven in before the gale, only to wash back to the great deep in silence. The calm is never of long duration, and no one is simple enough to think that the storm is over.

At first men were afraid of the tempest. The Eastern Question was a constant dread; but now, becoming accustomed to the fickle sky, the matter is treated as one of the every-day occurrences. Indeed, the more reckless ones even defy the threatened danger. Instead of restraining the ambitious leaders, the common people have besought their respective governments to run the risk of war, and have even demanded that they should face the peril, in order to rid the world of the dark presence. And yet the issue does not come; it seems impossible to make it come, although the trigger is so nicely poised that a mere touch will discharge the shot that means so much to the nations. In covert terms men even pray for war; they tell us it is a righteous cause; that God is angry because the Christian nations do not speak out, and stop the bloody Turk. They wonder that the goaded nations do not move.

Is not the situation strange? What is the secret? Is it due to some dark intrigue between the wily sultan and his seeming foes? — No; it is not this. The Bible gives the answer: *The Israel of God are not yet sealed!* He says, "*Hold the winds.*" In vain do men pray and preach for the die to be cast. With impunity the victims are slaughtered; the world is aroused. Men want to fight; but they cannot begin; for the Lord says, Hold the elements a little longer.

But does not the Lord care for the sufferings of

the helpless men and women, and for little children that perish?—Yes, he marks their groans and tears. He cares for all the world, and gladly would he have them spared. In infinite pity, he is now letting a few drops fall, in order that all may heed his invitation to seek shelter before the fearful roar of the tornado is upon them. When it comes, the ruin will be, not a single province, nor a single nation, but a world. And will men hear, and turn, and escape?—Yes; a few true Israelites are still in the land, and not a war dog can be loosed until they are gathered and sealed. Quickly the message must now go to all, in every land, who may be reached. The seal of the living God must be placed upon their brow, and for them the armies of earth must wait. Proud kings cannot move until the humble saint has passed from the danger of this world under the sheltering wings of the Almighty. True Israel, the remnant of the blood-washed throng, must be searched out and sealed in their foreheads. When this is done, the winds will blow from all quarters, and form the great whirlwind spoken of in the Scriptures of truth:—

Thus saith the Lord of Hosts, Behold, evil shall go forth from nation to nation, and a great whirlwind shall be raised up from the coasts of the earth. And the slain of the Lord shall be at that day from one end of the earth even unto the other end of the earth; they shall not be lamented, neither gathered, nor buried; they shall be dung upon the ground.[1]

[1] Jer. 25: 32, 33.

ELIJAH THE PROPHET.

Another prophecy shows the fact that God's judgments will not come upon the world until the warning has been sounded: —

Behold, I will send you Elijah the prophet before the coming of the great and dreadful day of the Lord.[1]

Just before the Messiah appeared among men, John the Baptist was sent as a special messenger to prepare the way of the Lord. He was not Elijah in person; but he came in the "spirit and power of Elias."[2] Christ said of him that "Elias is come already, and they knew him not."[3] Those who received his message were prepared to recognize the "Lamb of God" when he appeared. John's message was one of denunciation upon those who thought their national descent was sufficient evidence that the blessing of Israel was theirs. He laid the ax at the root of the tree, and warned them that, notwithstanding their great profession, they were not truly Abraham's seed. Only by sincere repentance could they know Him that stood among them. Elias had come; but they knew him not. Neither did they know him of whom John spoke; for they beheaded one, and crucified the other.

A similar condition will exist just before the "great and dreadful day of the Lord." Nations will again boast of their Christianity, or even claim

---

[1] Mal. 4: 5. [2] Luke 1: 17. [3] Matt. 17: 12.

to be "lost Israel," and heirs to the kingdom of David, while they are not ready for the winds to blow. Therefore another message must go in the spirit and power of Elijah to awaken the deluded people. The time has come for the message; the conditions are parallel with those of old; true Israel will recognize the truth, and be sealed with the seal of God. The world knows them not. They are "lost" in the eyes of men, and yet they are princes of God and heirs with Christ to David's throne. Even now the nations are waiting for them to come into the ark; but they know not the pilgrim band.

THE EVERLASTING GOSPEL.

A third time the Lord has pointed to his people in the midst of the nations, and, symbolized by his messengers, the angels, they give the final invitation and warning: —

And I saw another angel fly in the midst of heaven, having the everlasting gospel to preach unto them that dwell on the earth, and to every nation, and kindred, and tongue, and people, saying with a loud voice, Fear God, and give glory to him; for the hour of his judgment is come: and worship him that made heaven, and earth, and the sea, and the fountains of waters.[1]

"The hour of his judgment"— this is the special burden of the last gospel invitation. Already our attention has been called to the closing work of our High Priest in cleansing the heavenly sanctuary, which ends the destiny of all men, and brings

[1] Rev. 14: 6, 7.

the decree which says, "He that is unjust, let him be unjust still: and he which is filthy, let him be filthy still: and he that is righteous, let him be righteous still: and he that is holy, let him be holy still."[1] Christ then makes the final atonement for the righteous, but blots out the names of those who do not overcome.

In these decisions, judgment is passed upon all cases. Therefore, in pointing the world to the true sanctuary, and the closing ministry of Christ for true Israel, the judgment hour is proclaimed. Think of it: the judgment in progress, and yet the world preparing war, and the church talking of a future age of peace and safety! Where is Elijah the prophet? Where is John the Baptist? Where is Luther or Wesley? Who shall declare before all the nations that the judgment has begun on the dead of past ages, and will soon come to the living? Men of faith are needed; for the lovers of pleasures more than lovers of God will ridicule the messenger and despise the message.

BABYLON IS FALLEN.

Another angel follows the first, and in sadness announces that "Babylon is fallen, is fallen, that great city, because she made all nations drink of the wine of the wrath of her fornication."[2] "Babylon the Great" is a family name,— that of mother and daughters who have taken the name of Christ, and yet have linked themselves with the wicked,

[1] Rev. 22: 11.   [2] Rev. 14: 8.

ambitious nations, even flaunting the title of their unlawful union in the expression, "Christian nation." The very name discloses the fact of a moral fall which has come to her who once leaned only on the arm of her beloved Lord.

THE LAST WARNING.

A third angel follows the first and second, and utters the final warning to all who worship the powers of earth. In terrible words he declares that the wine of the wrath of God is about to be poured out without mixture into the cup of his indignation.[1] This includes the seven last plagues; for "in them is filled up the wrath of God." Without entering into the details of these warning messages, no one can fail to see something of their nature from this short outline. As surely as there is an Eastern Question before the world, calling men to the battle of the great day of God, there is a warning and an entreaty sent in love to all who are exposed to danger, that they may escape the snare, and stand before the Son of Man.

The reader is requested to stop and ponder on this matter. Reason alone teaches that a crisis must ultimately come over matters in the East. For this expected event the armies are drilled and maintained. From a score of Bible prophecies we learn that this struggle will culminate in the destruction of all nations, close the day of God's grace, and usher in the day of his wrath. In spite

[1] Rev. 14 : 9-12.

of the fears, and even the hopes, that some decisive action will settle existing complications, a certain degree of peace is yet granted, and this very holding of the winds, we are told, is in order that God's servants may be sealed, ready for their redemption. This is in accordance with the deliverance promised to all whose names are in the book when the "time of trouble" spoken of by Daniel the prophet shall come. Thus in the midst of the distress already coming upon the world, the Lord remembers his "little flock," the lost sheep of the house of Israel. They are found in every nation and of every creed; and so the "everlasting gospel" is once more sent to all mankind, announcing that the hour of God's judgment is come. Christ is entered into the most holy place of the sanctuary, to confess the names of his people; and when this is accomplished, his work as priest will be done; the mystery of God in the gospel will be finished, and the day of the Lord begin, bringing his unmixed wrath.

But, alas! the truth which is sent to shelter the people, is not in accordance with popular ideas. They are expecting Christ to reign as king in this world, even as the ancient Jews looked for a Messiah to set up the kingdom at Jerusalem. As did the Jews of old, they regard themselves as the favored people of the Lord, notwithstanding their lives show that they have only a form of godliness. They refuse the warning which bids them worship

Him that made all things, but cling more closely to the civil powers for protection. They reject the law of God, but strain at gnats in conforming to traditions of the fathers. What excuse can they make when the King comes in to see the guests? They will be "speechless." Having been miserably deceived, now they must suffer the consequences.

Thank God! a few will know the call of the Good Shepherd. His sheep know his voice. No Babel of tongues can drown the sound of the Master's well-known tones. God's people are coming. Out of each tribe, God enrolls the names of those who have kept his commandments and the faith of Jesus, — a little company to be added to the great multitude of preceding generations, — just a remnant, but enough to make up the number; and "so all Israel shall be saved," and a voice from the throne will declare, "It is done."

Happy is the man whom his Lord shall own in that day. No plague shall come upon those who have the seal of God in their foreheads. They are marked with the divine stamp. Like the blood of the passover lamb on the door-posts of Israel when the angel of death went through Egypt, will be the seal of God on the brow of his saints. They are passed over by the vials of destruction, "left" unharmed, while the wicked are "taken," as the "eagles" devour the loathsome "carcass." Then follows the coming of Christ in person, to receive his waiting, trusting, loving Israel.

Chapter Fifteen.

THE SECOND EXODUS.

"NOW all these things happened unto them for ensamples: and they are written for our admonition, upon whom the ends of the world are come."[1] No further proof is needed to show the relation sustained between the national Israel and the true Israel in these last days. They were the type; these the antitype. They were the pattern; these the original.

God teaches the world by object-lessons. When he would make known his invisible power to create righteous men where only sin had previously reigned, he brought a visible world out of primeval chaos. Thus his eternal power and Godhead are revealed in the works of nature. When he would point penitent men to the Divine Sacrifice, he gave them the lesson in the innocent victims of the ceremonial system. When he would shadow forth the mediatorial service of the great High Priest in heaven, the Levitical priesthood was ordained. When he would show the divisions in Christ's ministry, he gave the figure of the worldly sanctuary, with its two apartments, each with its appointed service. When he would teach men of

[1] 1 Cor. 10:11.

the final load of guilt that will be laid on Satan, he directed that the scapegoat should bear away the sins of the people. When he would represent his true people Israel, unknown and persecuted by the proud world, he showed it by the Hebrews' bondage in Egypt. When he would illustrate the final wrath upon the nations, he poured out his plagues on Pharaoh. When he would reveal the deliverance of his saints, he brought Israel out of bondage. When he would typify the new earth, he brought his people to a land flowing with milk and honey. When he would point them to the New Jerusalem above, he brought them to the earthly "city of peace." When he would describe the glory of the world to come, he used the kingdom under the reign of David and Solomon. When he would show the consequences of pride and disobedience, he destroyed the host brought out of Egypt, sent their posterity into captivity, cursed their land, burned up their city, and finally scattered them over the earth as a constant witness of their folly.

From this rapid survey of the field we now return to the point where the national Israel was discarded, and the gospel went to all nations. To the church as thus constituted was committed the gospel work of teaching the nature, extent, duration, and glory of the future kingdom of God. Their task will last until the gospel work is done; so from the very nature of the case, they cannot enter upon their final rest until probation is ended.

THE DISPERSION.

It was not the Master's plan that his disciples should stay at Jerusalem, and wait for the nations to come to them for truth; but the command was, "Go ye into all the world, and preach the gospel to every creature." The harvest is great, and the laborers are few; therefore the people of God were to be dispersed throughout all the world, as missionaries to those who sit in darkness. Thus, again, we see that there can be no gathering of Israel until after the gospel to sinners is finished. Persecution is one means by which the gospel message has been carried to earth's remotest bounds. Immediately after the stoning of Stephen, the dispersion began, as shown by the following words:—

And Saul was consenting unto his death. And at that time there was a great persecution against the church which was at Jerusalem; and they were all scattered abroad throughout the regions of Judea and Samaria, except the apostles. . . . Therefore they that were scattered abroad went everywhere preaching the word.[1]

The time had come for national lines in gospel work to be broken down, and God's messengers were to realize that with him there is no respect of persons. And yet every individual who accepts the message is a true Israelite. No tribes are lost in the registry of God; but in the sight of men they are lost, simply because the marks of a true Jew are known only to God. In this sense James addressed his epistle:—

[1] Acts 8 : 1-4.

James, a servant of God and of the Lord Jesus Christ, to the *twelve tribes which are scattered abroad*, greeting. My brethren, count it all joy when ye fall into divers temptations.[1]

James was a Christian, writing to Christian brethren, yet he calls them the twelve tribes. He understood perfectly well that all true followers of Jesus are Israelites indeed. He also recognized the fact that *no tribes are lost.* Twelve, the original number, were in existence in A. D. 60, when he wrote, but they were scattered abroad, and suffering "divers temptations." It is not the lot of Israel to be honored in this world. Christ, the King of Israel, suffered persecution and death, and he assures his followers that the same treatment will be theirs also. The very enthusiasm now manifested in behalf of the national Israel is evidence that little is known concerning true Israel even in "Christian lands." John in holy vision saw the "one hundred and forty and four thousand of all the tribes of the children of Israel," for whose sake the "four winds" are now held, and heard his angel guide describe their experience in these closing days: "These are they which came out of great tribulation, and have washed their robes, and made them white in the blood of the Lamb."[2]

As surely as the Eastern Question is even now demanding the attention of the nations, as surely as God is even now holding the winds, so surely are the remnant of true Israel now being sealed

---

[1] James 1:1.   [2] Rev. 7:14.

with the seal of the living God. And yet, in harmony with true Israel in the days of Abraham and Christ, the peculiar features of their faith and practise expose them to the ridicule of men and the oppression of unjust civil laws. Thus they will come up out of great tribulation. This will be seen more clearly by another description of them:—

> And the dragon was wroth with the woman, and went to make war with the remuant of her seed, which keep the commandments of God, and have the testimony of Jesus Christ.[1]

The "woman" is evidently a symbol of the true church in all ages. The "remnant of her seed" must be true Christians in the last days. The "dragon" is Satan (verse 9), who works through human beings. "War," in this case, is persecution, under the sanction of religious and civil laws, rather than warfare in the usual acceptation of the term. The reason for this hostility is that the "remnant" "keep the commandments of God." They must also be true Christians; for they "have the testimony of Jesus Christ."

Now can any one imagine how a people who are truly Christians in these days can be singular in reference to the commandments of God? Suppose a comparatively small number — not more than 144,000 — should be convinced that the seventh day of the week is the Sabbath, just as the fourth commandment in God's law declares it to be; would they not immediately be considered "odd," and

[1] Rev. 12:17.

even "fanatical" or "crazy," by the millions of people who regard Sunday, the first day of the week, as the Lord's day? We need not argue whether they are right or wrong in this practise; the question is, How would they be regarded by the rest of the world? Is it not certain that they would be ridiculed and despised by other religious bodies? Would they not also come in conflict with the laws of civil governments which require that Sunday shall be observed as a sacred rest day? Is it not a fact that nations the most devoutly religious in the popular honor they bestow upon Sunday, would thus become the foremost persecutors against those who should keep Jehovah's Sabbath? In the very nature of the case, would not the conscientious minority be obliged to suffer at the hands of the majority? Here would certainly be sufficient ground for religious prejudice and bigotry to oppress the few who differed so radically on such a vital matter.

It cannot be denied that the keeping of the seventh or last day of the week is according to the explicit commandment of God, even though many for various reasons decide that another day will answer the purpose. The Sabbath was given to Israel for the express purpose of being a "sign" between them and the Lord.[1] Christ declared that he did not come to destroy a jot or tittle of the law; and do not all Christians believe in the eternal obligation of the ten commandments? Then is it

---

[1] Ex. 31:13.

not a Christian duty to keep the Sabbath? And if true Christians are really true Israelites, Abraham's seed in Christ, will they not keep the day honored by both Abraham and Christ? In other words, when God shall once more prepare to manifest his true Israel before the world, will not the original Sabbath be a "seal in their foreheads"? If these suppositions are correct, will not the discovery of "lost Israel" bring to view a company of *Christian Sabbath-keepers?* Would not this mark identify them with Israel of old, from Adam to Christ, who by faith trusted in Christ for grace to keep the law of God?

As we have found only one gospel for all the race during the different ages; only one Saviour for Jew and Gentile alike; only one divine law, written in our hearts, is there not really one Sabbath — the seventh day — for all men? If since she "fled into the wilderness," the "woman" — the church — has lost this memorial of the creative work wrought out by Christ and the Father, is it not reasonable to suppose that it will be restored to her when she again comes up from the wilderness leaning on the arm of her Beloved? If the people of God in the last generation are found following closely the gospel of Christ, while keeping the Sabbath that he kept and commanded, will they be recognized by those who look for the return of Israel? Or will the very fact that they do keep the Sabbath, cause them to be despised and rejected, as was their Master? If the Jews could not recognize their own Messiah, for whom they looked, because he came not according to their traditions, will those who now have so deep an interest in his elect people, Israel, receive them while keeping the commandments of God instead of the traditions of the church?

John saw again the same remnant of Christian Israel proclaiming the last warnings to all the world, as recorded in Rev. 14:6–12, and instantly recognized them as true Israel in affliction:—

> Here is the patience of the saints: here are they that keep the commandments of God, and the faith of Jesus.

They are the ones who point out the closing work of Christ as priest in the cleansing of the heavenly sanctuary, and show that the hour of judgment is come; they also point out the dangers which threaten a careless world in Babylon; they tell of the impending close of probation, and the pouring out of the wine of the wrath of God in the seven last plagues; they know that the coming of Christ is near, and that the gathering calamities involved in the Eastern Question are waiting to break over the world. Knowing these facts, they pray for the winds to be held, while they hasten to tell the world, searching out the lost Israel of God, that all may receive his seal, and escape the raging storm. They are Jews inwardly, the living remnant of true Israel.

THE SECOND EXODUS. 235

And a work of this kind is now in progress among the nations of earth. A people have lately arisen who are calling special attention to these very matters. They claim to be giving the messages found in the prophecies just quoted. Their motto is, "The commandments of God, and the faith of Jesus." While trusting to Christ for justification and sanctification, they are strict observers of the precepts of Jehovah, including the Sabbath of the fourth commandment. It is superfluous to add that on account of their faith and practise, they are exposed to business losses, ridicule of friends, and even imprisonment and fines. But the careful student of the Scriptures will notice that these marks of unpopularity are perfectly consistent with the character of true Israelites. No doubt these people will soon become widely known, and already their missionaries are in every land, and their literature is extensively circulated in more than thirty languages.

It is at least a remarkable coincidence that a body holding the peculiar doctrines committed to true Israel is in existence, with about 50,000 adherents, and numbers constantly increasing, at the very time when so much is said about the return of the Hebrew nation; and when this movement is connected with the drying up of the Turkish Empire, gigantic preparations for war, the holding of the impending struggle notwithstanding the demand for the Turk's summary punishment, and over all an Eastern Question of thrilling interest. Each actor in this world's last drama is already on the stage; and it behooves each one of us to discern the signs of the times. Already we have learned that the winds are stayed in order that the remnant of Israel may be sealed with the sign of the living God. Is the calling out of a people to keep the Sabbath committed to Israel a fulfilment of this prophecy? Surely if such is the case, these people are not recognized in the world to-day as the chosen seed of Abraham.

GATHERING ISRAEL.

Having rapidly sketched the scattering of true Israel, their work among all the nations, the remnant now being called by the special message of the gospel, their bondage and persecution, we now come to their final deliverance from the oppressor's hand,— the *second exodus*, the jubilee, the gathering together of all the people of God in their permanent home. Let us read a few of the promises on this point:—

And one of them, named Caiaphas, being the high priest that same year, said unto them, Ye know nothing at all, nor consider that it is expedient for us that one man should die for the people, and that the whole nation perish not. And this spake he not of himself: but being high priest that year, he prophesied that Jesus should die for that nation; and not for that nation only, but that also he should gather together in one the children of God that were scattered abroad.[1]

1 John 11 : 49-52.

From this we learn that the gathering of Israel is the great consummation. Through Isaiah the same thing is foretold: —

And it shall come to pass in that day, that the Lord shall set his hand again the second time to recover the remnant of his people, which shall be left, from Assyria, and from Egypt, and from Pathros, and from Cush, and from Elam, and from Shinar, and from Hamath, and from the islands of the sea. And he shall set up an ensign for the nations, and shall assemble the outcasts of Israel, and gather together the dispersed of Judah from the four corners of the earth.[1]

Also in Jeremiah: —

Therefore, behold, the days come, saith the Lord, that it shall no more be said, The Lord liveth, that brought up the children of Israel out of the land of Egypt: but, The Lord liveth, that brought up the children of Israel from the land of the north, and from all the lands whither he had driven them; and I will bring them again into their land that I gave unto their fathers.[2]

Probably all will agree that these promises pertain to the future, and therefore they must apply to true Israel; for no such gathering of the Hebrew nation will take place. The language is very positive, and the event will far exceed any previous manifestation of divine power.

Oh that the salvation of Israel were come out of Zion! when the Lord bringeth back the captivity of his people, Jacob shall rejoice, and Israel shall be glad.[3]

[1] Isa. 11:11, 12.   [2] Jer. 16:14, 15.   [3] Ps. 14:7.

THE TIME OF ISRAEL'S RETURN.

No attempt will be made to fix an exact date for the gathering of God's people; for the Saviour said to the disciples who wished to know the time of the restoration of the kingdom to Israel, "It is not for you to know the times or the seasons, which the Father hath put in his own power."[1] The time when the fulfilment of the promises draws near may, however, be learned from the relation of this to other events. Enough has already been said to show that Israel will not be gathered until their work of teaching the gospel to every creature is done. This will be the close of human probation, and will leave the wicked without excuse when the seven last plagues are poured out. The next event is the coming of Christ to gather his people Israel:—

And they shall see the Son of Man coming in the clouds of heaven with power and great glory. And he shall send his angels with a great sound of a trumpet, and they shall gather together his elect from the four winds, from one end of heaven to the other.[2]

This not only fixes the gathering of Israel at Christ's coming, but it also shows in what way the people of God are assembled. No railroads or steamboats are needed; but "angels, that excel in strength," and who run and return "as the appearance of a flash of lightning," will transport the scattered saints of God from the most distant parts

---

[1] Acts 1:6, 7.   [2] Matt. 24:30, 31.

of the earth to meet their Lord and King. This is the only "gathering of Israel," or "return of the Jews," which this world will ever witness. This gathering is in perfect harmony with all the Bible teaches concerning the true Israel and the time and place of their inheritance.

THE RIGHTEOUS DEAD.

Another fact of tremendous importance and thrilling interest in connection with the gathering of true Israel, is that all the righteous dead, as well as all the righteous who remain alive, are included in the promised return. God will not gather some of Israel, and leave the rest behind. By far the larger portion who are worthy to bear that honored title, have gone down in death. Abraham, Isaac, and Jacob are dead; and their righteous seed have likewise "died in faith, not having received the promises, but having seen them afar off, and were persuaded of them, and embraced them, and confessed that they were strangers and pilgrims on the earth."[1] What shall be done with these? Are they not to share in the promises which cheered their fainting hearts when buffeted by a world which knew them not? Long they have waited in the silent tomb for the "jubilee" trumpet to sound the hour of their release from the bondage of death. An "example" of this is recorded in the dying request of Joseph:—

[1] Heb. 11:13.

By faith Joseph, when he died, made mention of the departing of the children of Israel; and gave commandment concerning his bones.[1]

An earthly Canaan was the promised land to this typical Israel, and the going forth of the living multitude from Egyptian bondage prefigured the second exodus, when the true Israel will come to the heavenly Canaan, and not a saint will be left behind. From the days of Abel until the end of time, the children of the promise have fallen by the cruel hand of death, many of them the martyrs of a faith which in each generation has aroused the anger of the dragon. Their bones line the highway from the gates of Eden lost to the gates of Eden restored. Who shall resuscitate these whitened relics of a godly race, and bear them, crowned with immortal life, to the city of God? Again we turn to the Scriptures for our answer:—

The hand of the Lord was upon me, and carried me out in the Spirit of the Lord, and set me down in the midst of the valley which was full of bones, and caused me to pass by them round about: and, behold, there were very many in the open valley; and, lo, they were very dry. And he said unto me, Son of Man, can these bones live? And I answered, O Lord God, thou knowest. Again he said unto me, Prophesy upon these bones, and say unto them, O ye dry bones, hear the word of the Lord. Thus saith the Lord God unto these bones: Behold, I will cause breath to enter into you, and ye shall live: and I will lay sinews upon you, and will bring up flesh upon you, and cover you with skin, and put breath in you, and ye shall live; and ye shall know that I am the Lord. So I prophesied as I was commanded:

[1] Heb. 11:22.

and as I prophesied, there was a noise, and behold a shaking, and the bones came together, bone to his bone. And when I beheld, lo, the sinews and the flesh came up upon them, and the skin covered them above: but there was no breath in them. Then said he unto me, Prophesy unto the wind, prophesy, son of man, and say to the wind, Thus saith the Lord God: Come from the four winds, O breath, and breathe upon these slain, that they may live. So I prophesied as he commanded me, and the breath came into them, and they lived, and stood up upon their feet, *an exceeding great army.*

Then he said unto me, Son of man, these bones are the whole house of Israel: behold, they say, Our bones are dried, and our hope is lost: we are cut off for our parts. Therefore prophesy and say unto them, Thus saith the Lord God: Behold, O my people, I will open your graves, and cause you to come up out of your graves, and *bring you into the land of Israel.* And ye shall know that I am the Lord, when I have opened your graves, O my people, and brought you up out of your graves, and shall put my spirit in you, and ye shall live, and *I shall place you in your own land:* then shall ye know that I the Lord have spoken it, and performed it, saith the Lord.[1]

No explanation of the foregoing words is needed. Our comments will be few, but the lesson is impressive. It is certain that the holy dead are a part of the Israel of God; and when the living enter the land of promise, those who have died will rise from their graves, and join the company. The living do not precede the dead, neither do the dead go before the living; all go at the same moment. These conclusions are precisely what the Bible elsewhere asserts: —

[1] Eze. 37 : 1-14.

And these all, having obtained a good report through faith, received not the promise: God having provided some better thing for us, that they without us should not be made perfect.[1]

Paul states the facts clearly, as follows: —

But I would not have you to be ignorant, brethren, concerning them which are asleep, that ye sorrow not, even as others which have no hope. For if we believe that Jesus died and rose again, even so them also which sleep in Jesus will God bring with him. For this we say unto you by the word of the Lord, that we which are alive and remain unto the coming of the Lord shall not prevent [go before] them which are asleep. For the Lord himself shall descend from heaven with a shout, with the voice of the archangel, and with the trump of God: and *the dead in Christ shall rise first: then we which are alive and remain shall be caught up together with them in the clouds, to meet the Lord in the air:* and so shall we ever be with the Lord. Wherefore comfort one another with these words.[2]

A proper consideration of these words of inspiration would dispel much of the confusion which now exists with reference to the time when the reward will be given; but the point now to be emphasized is that at the coming of Christ the righteous dead are raised, and join the living saints in the grand exodus to the "Holy Land." None are caught up before that event, and none are gathered afterward; but all go together. The redeemed will not be a succession of straggling bands, but an "exceeding great army," composed of those who come up from the opened graves, together with the living "remnant."

---

[1] Heb. 11:39, 40.   [2] 1 Thess. 4:13-18.

THE FINAL CHANGE.

One more link in the chain of truth can now be coupled with what has gone before; namely, at the coming of Christ, a physical change must pass upon all the righteous, before they can enter upon the inheritance. No person in the present mortal body can possibly enter the promised land. If this point is clearly taught in the Scriptures, it will again show that the kingdom of Christ will not be set up in this present world, where death reigns; for no human being, as now constituted, could live upon it. Every individual must be "changed" in his physical composition before he is removed to his eternal possessions. Paul is speaking of the resurrection body, and he says: —

> So also is the resurrection of the dead. It is sown in corruption: it is raised in incorruption: it is sown in dishonor; it is raised in glory: it is sown in weakness; it is raised in power: it is sown a natural body; it is raised a spiritual body. . . . Now this I say, brethren, that flesh and blood cannot inherit the kingdom of God; neither doth corruption inherit incorruption. Behold, I show you a mystery: We shall not all sleep, *but we shall all be changed*, in a moment, in the twinkling of an eye, at the last trump: for the trumpet shall sound, and the dead shall be raised incorruptible, and we shall be changed. For this corruptible must put on incorruption, and this mortal must put on immortality. [1]

Christ's kingdom will have no end; it is an incorruptible, eternal reign on the throne of David.

---
[1] 1 Cor. 15:42-53.

Nothing subject to death and decay will enter that world; hence, when the Lord appears, the mortal bodies of all the redeemed will be changed for immortal, spiritual bodies. The blood is the life of these mortal bodies; the immortal bodies will be spiritual. But the spiritual body will be as literal as the bodies we now possess. Christ, after his resurrection, had flesh and bones, hands, feet, etc. His disciples saw, handled, and heard him. He ate food, walked, talked, and did other physical acts. He was not a phantom, nor a disembodied, immaterial spirit. He ascended up to heaven in a tangible bodily form, and now sits at the right hand of God as the *man* Christ Jesus. When he comes again, every true Israelite, every Christian, will be made like him in outward form: —

For our conversation is in heaven; from whence also we look for the Saviour, the Lord Jesus Christ; who shall change our vile body, that it may be fashioned like unto his glorious body, according to the working whereby he is able even to subdue all things unto himself.[1]

No man can endure the glory of Christ's personal presence without this wonderful change in his physical frame; and so it will be impossible for sinful, mortal individuals to enter the kingdom: —

For this ye know, that no whoremonger, nor unclean person, nor covetous man, who is an idolater, hath any inheritance in the kingdom of Christ and of God.[2]

[1] Phil. 3:20, 21.   [2] Eph. 5:5.

THE SECOND EXODUS.

This fact alone is sufficient to show that no work of conversion for wicked men or evil angels can possibly take place after Christ takes his kingdom. Only those who in this life are made new creatures in heart, will receive the new body at the sounding of the last trump. Then an instantaneous change will pass on all the redeemed Israel. God has shown in vision the end of that people whom he has chosen: —

How shall I curse, whom God hath not cursed? or how shall I defy, whom the Lord hath not defied? For from the top of the rocks I see him, and from the hills I behold him: lo, the people shall dwell alone, and shall not be reckoned among the nations. Who can count the dust of Jacob, and the number of the fourth part of Israel? Let me die the death of the righteous, and let my last end be like his.[1]

If a man die, shall he live again? all the days of my appointed time will I wait, till my change come. Thou shalt call, and I will answer thee: thou wilt have a desire to the work of thine hands.[2]

For I know that my Redeemer liveth, and that he shall stand at the latter day upon the earth: and though after my skin worms destroy this body, yet in my flesh shall I see God: whom I shall see for myself, and mine eyes shall behold, and not another; though my reins be consumed within me.[3]

O, what a happy day will that be for all Israel, when their Redeemer comes to earth again to "change" his waiting saints! He will call them forth from the silent tomb and from the living multitude; and together they will meet in the air.

[1] Num. 23:8-10. [2] Job 14:14, 15. [3] Job 19:25-27.

Before closing this special topic, we invite the reader to survey the whole field over which we have thus far passed, and note the perfect harmony. Each part naturally blends with the rest. All is plain, and each text has its proper place. We began with the first mention of the name "Israel." We have followed the history of the people who bear this name through obscurity and persecution, and now we have seen them leave this world forever, caught up to the Lord. Another world opens before them, and we follow still.

Chapter Sixteen.

THE MILLENNIUM.

THE word "millennium" means one thousand years without respect to conditions which may exist during that period; but in common use it has come to denote a time of universal peace and happiness on this earth. Whether or not this general expectation will be realized, must be learned from the Scriptures; popular use proves nothing. The word does not occur in the Bible; but a period of time of that length is described in Revelation 20, a portion of which chapter we will examine: —

And I saw an angel come down from heaven, having the key of the bottomless pit and a great chain in his hand. And he laid hold on the dragon, that old serpent, which is the devil, and Satan, and bound him a thousand years, and cast him into the bottomless pit, and shut him up, and set a seal upon him, that he should deceive the nations no more, till the thousand years should be fulfilled: and after that he must be loosed a little season. And I saw thrones, and they sat upon them, and judgment was given unto them; . . . and they lived and reigned with Christ a thousand years. But the rest of the dead lived not again until the thousand years were finished. This is the first resurrection. Blessed and holy is he that hath part in the first resurrection: on such the second death hath no power, but they shall be priests of God and of Christ, and shall reign with him a thousand years. And when the thousand years are expired, Satan shall be loosed out of his prison, and shall go out to deceive the nations which are in the four quarters of the earth, Gog and Magog, to gather them together to battle: the number of whom is as the sand of the sea.

This language is understood by many to mean that Christ will establish his kingdom in this world at Jerusalem, and so bind Satan that the restored nation of Israel will be converted, and then the gospel will extend to the Gentile nations during a thousand years of peace and happiness. Overwhelming evidence has already been presented to show that much of this theory is false. From the harmony in numerous texts of Scripture, on a dozen or more independent lines, it has been found that this entire fabric is built on sand. The same conclusion will again be reached in a still more decided manner.

THE TWO RESURRECTIONS.

It will be noticed in the foregoing quotation that the thousand years are preceded by a resurrection of the "blessed and holy," and followed by another resurrection for the "rest of the dead." This shows that there will be two resurrections, separated by an interval of a thousand years. The two classes mentioned include the entire human race. All the righteous come up at the beginning of the millennium, and all the wicked at its close. Both classes will rise again, but not at the same time. This difference in time is taught in several other texts. Christ spoke of some who "shall be accounted worthy to obtain that world, and the resurrection from the dead." [1] If there were but one resurrection for the entire race, no previous investigation would be needed to determine who were worthy; but with the idea of two resurrections, his words are easily understood. Paul, too, spoke of his great desire to "attain unto the resurrection of the dead." [2] As he distinctly states that both the just and the unjust will be raised, his anxiety must have been to come up with the "blessed and holy" in the first resurrection. He also spoke of the ancient worthies who died in faith of a "better resurrection."

In regard to the time when the first resurrection occurs, we have already learned that when Christ comes, the holy of all ages who sleep in Jesus will come out of their graves, immortal; and as this is also at the beginning of the thousand years, we know that the millennium will begin when the Lord appears, and continue until the rest of the dead are raised, when the thousand years are past. The order in the resurrection is thus stated by Paul: —

> For as in Adam all die, even so in Christ shall all be made alive. But every man in his own order: Christ the first-fruits; afterward they that are Christ's at his coming.[3]

[1] Luke 20:35. [2] Phil. 3:11. [3] 1 Cor. 15:22, 23.

But not only will the holy dead rise at the coming of the Lord, but those also that are alive will be changed to immortality at the same time, and all together they will be caught up to meet the Lord in the air. Therefore the millennium begins with every righteous person removed from this earth.

THE INHERITANCE IN HEAVEN.

Our next inquiry is, Where do Christ and the true Israel spend the one thousand years of the millennium? Do they remain in the air? Do they descend again upon the earth? Do they proceed upward to heaven? We have already learned that this earth is to pass away in a flood of fire, to be replaced by a new earth, a heavenly country, where Abraham and all Israel will eternally dwell; but this does not conflict with a stay of a thousand years in heaven, in case we find evidence to this effect. And this is exactly what we do find. Shortly before Christ went away, he said to the disciples: —

> Little children, yet a little while I am with you. Ye shall seek me: and as I said unto the Jews, Whither I go ye cannot come; so now I say to you. . . . Simon Peter said unto him, Lord, whither goest thou? Jesus answered him, Whither I go, thou canst not follow me now; but thou shalt follow me afterwards.[1]

There can be no doubt as to the place where Christ was going; for a little later he said, "But now I go my way to Him that sent me;" and again, "I go unto my Father." Therefore it is certain

---
[1] John 13:33, 36.

that the followers of Christ will sometime be taken to heaven and to the Father. He next tells the exact time when they will have this privilege:—

> Let not your heart be troubled: ye believe in God, believe also in me. In my Father's house are many mansions: if it were not so, I would have told you. I go to prepare a place for you. And if I go and prepare a place for you, *I will come again*, and receive you unto myself; that where I am, there ye may be also.[1]

This settles the matter conclusively; when Christ comes, all the righteous are taken to heaven. Peter, who wished to go with Christ at once, understood the promise of a future reward in heaven when the Lord returned; for he says:—

> Blessed be the God and Father of our Lord Jesus Christ, which according to his abundant mercy hath begotten us again unto a lively hope by the resurrection of Jesus Christ from the dead, to an inheritance incorruptible, and undefiled, and that fadeth not away, reserved in heaven for you.[2]

From all these texts we learn that a portion of Israel's inheritance is in heaven, and there they first proceed after being gathered out of this world to meet the Lord in the air. They do not stay in the air, neither do they immediately descend to the earth; but they go to the Father, where Jesus went. *Jerusalem*, the city of their hopes and treasures, is there. That is the city which Abraham saw, having twelve foundations. That is the capital

---

[1] John 14 : 1–3.   [2] 1 Peter 1 : 3, 4.

of Christ's kingdom, and the place where he will take the throne of David. There the redeemed host will gather, in the Father's kingdom, for the marriage supper of the Lamb. There is the place which Christ is now preparing for the return of Israel. Is it not strange that men have so lost sight of true Israel, the true inheritance, and the true city, that they think all is to be accomplished by the Jews' being gathered back to barren Judea and to dilapidated old Jerusalem? Instead of Israel's being gathered to any part of this world, they are removed to the central point in the universe, even to heaven. They will be removed as far from this earth as heaven is distant in space; and the difference between the two illustrates how far the whole theory devised by men is from the truth of God. How long do they stay in heaven? Do they come back at any time during the thousand years? These questions will be answered by a few plain facts.

JUDGING THE WORLD.

We are told just what the Israel of God will do during the entire millennium; they reign with Christ on thrones of judgment. Who are they judging? Paul answers: —

> Do ye not know that the saints shall judge the world? . . . Know ye not that we shall judge angels? how much more things that pertain to this life?[1]

Wicked men and evil angels will be judged during the millennium. Instead of a second probation

---

[1] 1 Cor. 6: 2, 3.

for these classes, it will be the period of their judicial examination and everlasting condemnation. Each case will be impartially tested, not with hope of pardon, but to apportion the relative degree of guilt. The saints are associated with Christ in that solemn tribunal. The wicked do not appear in person before the bar of God; for they are dead upon the earth, waiting for the second resurrection, at the close of the thousand years; but their *record* is written in the books in heaven, and from these faithfully kept volumes the testimony will be produced. Thus it is written: —

And I saw the dead, small and great, stand before God; and the books were opened: and another book was opened, which is the book of life: and the dead were judged out of those things which were written in the books, according to their works.[1]

As the "books" are in heaven, the judgment work must be carried on in the same place during the thousand years. Therefore the saints remain in heaven during the entire millennium, and there is not a righteous person on the earth during all that thousand years. This conclusion is unavoidable from the explicit statements of the Bible; but it is so much at variance with popular theories that the reader is invited to dwell a moment longer on the contrast. Instead of the wicked being alive during the millennium, they are all dead on the earth; instead of a second probation; it is a time of passing sentence on the lost; instead of "another

[1] Rev. 20 : 12.

gospel" being preached, there will not be a sound from human lips; instead of Christ and the true Israel being in Palestine at Jerusalem, they will be in heaven, within the New Jerusalem; instead of its being the time when the earth will be renewed, it is the period when it will be swept with the besom of destruction. It will be a time of "peace" to the warring nations; but it will be the hush of death. Under the fury of demons leading to the fray, the problem of the Eastern Question will have been solved; the battle of the great day of God Almighty will then be over; the whirlwind's work of death will be done; the seven last plagues will then have been poured out; and the remnant of the wicked will have been consumed by the glory of Christ's appearing. Not a man will be left alive.

THE EARTH DESOLATE.

In the very nature of the case, the earth will be utterly desolate during the millennium; for the righteous are in heaven, and the wicked are dead on the earth. The Bible testimony on this point is abundant and decisive: —

I beheld the earth, and, lo, it was without form, and void; and the heavens, and they had no light. I beheld the mountains, and, lo, they trembled, and all the hills moved lightly. I beheld, and, lo, *there was no man*, and all the birds of the heavens were fled. I beheld, and, lo, the fruitful place was a wilderness, and all the cities thereof were broken down at the presence of the Lord, and by his fierce anger. For thus hath the Lord said, The whole land shall be desolate; yet will I not make a full end. For this shall the earth mourn, and the heavens above be black: because I have spoken it, I have purposed it, and will not repent, neither will I turn back from it.[1]

Behold, the day of the Lord cometh, cruel both with wrath and fierce anger, to lay the land desolate; and he shall destroy the sinners thereof out of it. . . . And I will punish the world for their evil, and the wicked for their iniquity; and I will cause the arrogancy of the proud to cease, and will lay low the haughtiness of the terrible. I will make a man more precious than fine gold; even a man than the golden wedge of Ophir. Therefore will I shake the heavens, and the earth shall remove out of her place, in the wrath of the Lord of Hosts, and in the day of his fierce anger.[2]

Behold, the Lord maketh the earth empty, and maketh it waste, and turneth it upside down, and scattereth abroad the inhabitants thereof. . . . The land shall be utterly emptied, and utterly spoiled; for the Lord hath spoken this word. . . . The earth is utterly broken down, the earth is clean dissolved, the earth is moved exceedingly. The earth shall reel to and fro like a drunkard, and shall be removed like a cottage; and the transgression thereof shall be heavy upon it; and it shall fall, and not rise again.[3]

These are descriptions of the earth in a desolate, chaotic condition, without a man upon it. No theory which ignores these passages is true. Sometime the world will be a vast charnel-house of death. This time cannot come *before* the millennium begins; for men will be living — planting and building — until the coming of the Lord. It cannot come *after* the millennium; for then the earth

[1] Jer. 4:23-28.   [2] Isa. 13:9-13.   [3] Isa. 24:1-20.

will be created anew, and so remain to all eternity. Thus we are shut up to the conclusion that the time when the earth will be in this condition is during the thousand years of the millennium. At that time, and no other, are the circumstances such as make possible a fulfilment of the predictions of the earth's desolation. With probation finished when Christ's work as priest is done; with the pouring out of the plagues, and the great earthquake; with the coming of Christ, and the fleeing away of the islands and disappearing of mountains at his presence; with the righteous dead called from the tomb, the righteous living changed, and both classes removed to heaven together; and with all the wicked dead waiting their doom at the end of the thousand years, everything is ready for the earth to reel and totter and fall, ruined by the transgression of the human race.

With this view there is harmony in the word of God. Every text has its appropriate place. Nothing is strained to fit a theory, but each line falls naturally into its true place. And in view of the truth concerning this matter, what blindness has seized the minds of men that they cannot discern the danger drawing near! They are longing and praying for the millennium to dawn, dreaming of the world's conversion in a future age, crying, "Peace and safety," while the gospel message still pleads, and the earth groans for the final scenes.

SATAN BOUND.

Perhaps some may not see how the binding of Satan is to be accomplished under the conditions that will exist during the thousand years. But it is the circumstances described that bind him. The earth itself is the "bottomless pit." It will be a desolate wilderness, without an inhabitant.

Here we find the great original scapegoat, typified in the work of the earthly sanctuary by the scapegoat led into an uninhabited land, bearing the sins of Israel. When the round of service was done, and once each year the sanctuary was cleansed by the atonement of the priest, the sins of the people were borne by the high priest and placed on the scapegoat, and he was then taken to the wilderness, and left to perish. So when Christ, our High Priest in the true sanctuary in heaven, shall finish his round of service "once for all," by cleansing the sanctuary, and confessing the names of his people, their sins will be laid on Satan, and he will be cast into a desolate, ruined world, without inhabitant, awaiting his final destruction at the end of the millennium, when the saints shall have judged him and his host of evil angels and wicked men. Can any one fail to see the harmony between the type and the original in these two pictures? But if the earth were not desolate during the thousand years, the comparison would not hold.

Notice, further, that as the goat sent away was not slain, so Satan is not destroyed when he is cast into the desolate earth, or the "bottomless pit;" for he is alive still when the thousand years are past. While all around him are dead, he, with his angels, is still alive. This part of his experience is foretold in Isa. 14 : 12–20, under the name of Lucifer, "fallen from heaven:" "But thou art cast out of the grave like an abominable branch. . . . Thou shalt not be joined with them in burial." While the great warriors of earth are all silent in their prison-house of death, Lucifer, who aspired to be above the Most High in the courts of heaven, is now "cast out," spurned even by the cruel grave. Earth refuses to cover the monster of her ruin. In the midst of the rocking, reeling, vomiting abyss, Satan is confined for a thousand years. He is bound by a "chain" of circumstances over which he has no control. The saints are in heaven, out of his reach; the wicked are dead. His hands are tied; he is bound. The former "covering cherub" is then a shrinking felon.

And yet over that age of misery and ruin to wicked men, desolation to earth, and divine judgment against sin, a glamour has been cast by the father of lies, until the world is deceived into expecting it to be a time of universal peace and joy. Could any one but a fallen Lucifer invent such a refuge of lies to hide his head, and could any one but a devil gloat over the fearful havoc to the souls of men caused by this pernicious theory? Even the insatiable grave ought to say "Enough;" for there are no more; hell and destruction ought to be "full," when they have swallowed up a world.

At last the millennium, so dreary to earth, will pass away. Long seems the time to mortal minds; but with God, compared with eternity, the reign of sin is but one tick of the great clock, one swing of the mighty pendulum which marks the ages. For an instant we close our eyes to shut out the fearful sight; but we open them again to gaze forever on the glory of the world to come. Even while the storm-cloud passes by, the Israel of God, in heaven, behold over the Father's throne the rainbow arch, the "bow of promise."

JUDGMENT EXECUTED.

The execution of the judgment rendered in the investigation of the books will take place at the close of the thousand years. For this purpose the saints of God accompany Christ to earth once more. Enoch, the seventh in descent from Adam, saw that distant day, and prophesied: "Behold, the Lord cometh with ten thousands of his saints, to execute judgment upon all."[1] That is the time when the words of Zechariah will be fulfilled:—

> His feet shall stand in that day upon the mount of Olives, which is before Jerusalem on the east, and the mount of Olives shall cleave in the midst thereof toward the east and

[1] Jude 14, 15.

toward the west, and there shall be a very great valley; and half of the mountain shall remove toward the north, and half of it toward the south.[1]

On this spot, especially prepared, the city of God, the New Jerusalem, which is now above, and which will be the home of the saints during the thousand years, will descend in majestic beauty, as lovely as a bride adorned for her husband. This will be the "camp of the saints," "the beloved city," where the final doom of the wicked will be witnessed.[2]

The voice of Christ is next heard, calling the wicked dead to arise. From their long sleep the mighty host come forth, just as they fell, flushed with the fire of war, feverish with pleasure's chase, mocking the claims of God. Their number is like the sand of the seashore. All the wicked, from the days of Cain to the close of probation, are in that throng. Again the rocking crust of earth trembles beneath the march of millions of men.

SATAN LOOSED.

Satan's enforced bondage is over "for a little season." While the wicked were dead, he was bound; but as soon as the nations come up at the close of the thousand years, he is loosed for his final effort against the Son of God. Again he deceives the victims of former snares. Notice how naturally and perfectly each portion of this scene is adapted to the remainder. The binding of Satan was the

[1] Zech. 14: 4.   [2] Rev. 20: 9.

result of certain causes; when the cause is removed, he is loosed again. But the common view of the millennium is encompassed with inconsistencies and incongruities. For instance, if the Lord can consistently bind Satan for a thousand years so that the world may be converted, why is he set at liberty again? Why not keep him bound? Again, if the thousand years are a time when Christ and Israel convert the world, what an outrageous climax it is to have the devil, in "a little season," succeed in leading the nations back under his power, ruining in a brief period much that the righteous have done in a thousand years. What an absurdity! Bind Satan so that people cannot do wrong, and call them converted to Christ; then loose Satan, and let the nations apostatize again; and this is the final result of the glorious millennium that so many are expecting! Away with the false theory. It does not agree with itself, much less with the truth of God.

THE SECOND DEATH.

Having deceived the wicked nations which come up from death, Satan marshals them to attack the camp of the saints, the beloved city. Then for the first and last time all the human race are brought together. Abraham, Isaac, Jacob, and all Israel are in the city; outside are the sorcerers, idolaters, murderers, and all who make or love a lie. The supreme moment comes. Despair seizes the rebel throng, and they weep, and mourn, and curse their fate. Fire comes down upon them from above, and the earth opens her inner chambers of liquid fire, until the dust becomes brimstone, and the waters pitch. Everything is melted by the intense heat. Here the root and branches of evil are burned up, and reduced to ashes. Now a "full end" is made of Satan and sin. "Affliction shall not rise up the second time."[1] The second death is the end of the curse which sin has caused. From that unconscious condition there is no resurrection. The punishment is eternal destruction.

Surrounded by billows of flame which consume the wicked like tow, the New Jerusalem will be as secure as was the ark in the days of Noah. Her inhabitants are safe, while they behold the reward of the wicked: —

Now will I rise, saith the Lord; now will I be exalted; now will I lift up myself. Ye shall conceive chaff, ye shall bring forth stubble: your breath, as fire, shall devour you. And the people shall be as the burnings of lime, as thorns cut up shall they be burned in the fire. Hear, ye that are afar off, what I have done; and, ye that are near, acknowledge my might. The sinners in Zion are afraid; fearfulness hath surprised the hypocrites. Who among us shall dwell with the devouring fire? who among us shall dwell with everlasting burnings?

Notice the answer: —

He that walketh righteously, and speaketh uprightly; he that despiseth the gain of oppressions, that shaketh his hands

[1] Nahum 1:9.

from holding of bribes, that stoppeth his ears from hearing of blood, and shutteth his eyes from seeing evil; he shall dwell on high: his place of defense shall be the munitions of rocks: bread shall be given him; his water shall be sure. Thine eyes shall see the King in his beauty; they shall behold the land that is very far off.[1]

Here is foretold a time when the righteous will safely dwell in the midst of fiery flames, while all the wicked are like stubble and thorns. These are the conditions which will exist at the close of the thousand years, when righteous Israel will be in the "beloved city," and the wicked suffer the second death in the lake of fire. "The land that is very far off" then becomes nigh; for we, "according to his promise, look for new heavens and a new earth, wherein dwelleth righteousness."[2] "Wait on the Lord, and keep his way, and he shall exalt thee to inherit the land: when the wicked are cut off, thou shalt see it."[3] God's promises to Israel are sure.

[1] Isa. 33:10-17.   [2] 2 Peter 3:13.   [3] Ps. 37:34.

Chapter Seventeen.

THE ROYAL FAMILY.

IN previous chapters we have traced the history of Israel as pilgrims and strangers in this world, unknown, despised, and persecuted in every age. They are known and owned of the Lord, but not of men. Especially will the "remnant," "which keep the commandments of God, and have the faith of Jesus," be rejected in the last days. In their stead, men will look for the restoration of the natural, national Israel, once rejected for unbelief. We have pointed out that the same reason for which God then scattered the nation is now urged in their behalf. Had he intended to save Israel because of their Hebrew descent, they would not have been rejected for believing this; but any one who observes closely the history of the Jews will see that national pride and self-righteousness prevented them from understanding or appreciating the character of God and his people. Their only salvation was in the power of God to circumcise their hearts, that they might fulfil the royal law of love. But they trusted in national prerogatives, and rejected Christ, the true King of Israel. He was meek and lowly in heart, while they were proud and stubborn.

They trusted in the nation, and rejected God. In mercy to them, God dashed their idol to the ground, in order that they might turn to him. He rejected the nation, with all its boasted privileges, to teach them that they had no hope in that direction while rejecting his grace in Christ. It was a terrible warning to all men against the theory of salvation by national birth; and to emphasize the lesson, they are scattered throughout the world, that all the nations may know the folly of such a hope. How could God more plainly show his displeasure against trusting in the flesh?

Is it not a marvel that so many men to-day have failed to learn the truth on this matter? They even try to convert the Jews to Christianity by the same doctrine that has been their curse for thousands of years,— trying to lead them to Christ through the idea of national superiority. The carnal heart loves that doctrine, and thus many will be "converted," and expect that at last they will be the exalted nation which was in the dreams of their fathers nineteen hundred years ago. The Jews would have believed on Christ then, if their national hopes could have been realized through him, and it is no wonder that they will be ready to accept him now in the same manner. But such an acceptance of Christ is not conversion. Those who seek him only as one who will exalt them before the world, are converted to the lie that caused their fall. Eternal ruin will be the result of the deception now set before them.

It brought partial blindness the first time, and it will bring total blindness the second time. God destroyed the nation, that individuals might be saved by faith; but when the individuals still trust in themselves instead of God, the only result possible will be the destruction of the individuals. And how can we show men who advocate these things their mistake? If it was wrong for the ancient Jews to trust in national salvation, it is wrong for their descendants now to believe it; and if it is wrong for them, it is also wrong for others to believe it for them; and if it is wrong for any one to believe it, there is nothing but evil in teaching it. And this is the truth of the matter. John the Baptist, Christ, and Paul tried in vain to turn the multitude away from the former delusion, so we despair of any marked success in trying to turn them from the latter delusion. But as a few then grasped the true hope and were saved, so now a few will recognize the truth and become Israelites indeed. All who seek salvation on national lines will miss it, and all who seek it by a new birth will find it. Both classes, the false and the true, are described in the following words to the typical church of Philadelphia: —

I know thy works: behold, I have set before thee an open door, and no man can shut it: for thou hast a little strength, and hast kept my word, and hast not denied my name. Behold, I will make them of the synagogue of Satan, *which say they are Jews, and are not, but do lie;* behold, I will make them to come and worship before thy feet, and to know that I have loved thee. Because thou hast kept the word of my patience, I also will keep thee from the hour of temptation, which shall come upon all the world, to try them that dwell upon the earth. Behold, I come quickly: hold that fast which thou hast, that no man take thy crown. Him that overcometh will I make a pillar in the temple of my God, and he shall go no more out: and I will write upon him the name of my God, and the name of the city of my God, *which is New Jerusalem*, which cometh down out of heaven from my God: and I will write upon him my new name.[1]

We have also followed the Israel of God to their inheritance reserved in heaven, where they reign with Christ in the New Jerusalem above, during the thousand years that follow the coming of Christ. There they behold the glory of God bestowed on Christ before the foundation of the world. Only those who "overcome" can enter that city of God and see his face. Those who "*say they are Jews, and are not*"—all who trust in natural birth—will then be left upon this ruined earth. They have looked to this world for their home during the millennium, and the Lord lets them have it. Men get what they choose. They can spend the millennium in the New Jerusalem in heaven; or they can spend it in a desolate, ruined world under the hush of death. God is "not ashamed" of those who choose the heavenly city; but he is ashamed of those who choose this world in which to spend the millennium; and their car-

[1] Rev. 3:8-12.

casses will fall in the wilderness, while the people of God, like Caleb and Joshua, will enter into the inheritance in heaven.

We have followed the true Israel as they descend with Christ in the holy city at the close of the thousand years, to execute judgment on the ungodly and clear the earth from the curse of sin. To them Christ will say, "Behold, I make all things new;" and there, before their wondering eyes, a new world created, will be their eternal home. In that new earth every promise to them concerning the land will be fulfilled. It will be a "heavenly" country, and yet it will be a literal world, peopled with literal beings redeemed out of all nations. Its glories are often described in human language, and illustrated by things of this world; but it is divine.

The city, too, the New Jerusalem, is a literal city, with walls of precious stones, in which are the names of the twelve apostles; with gates of solid pearl, in which are engraved the names of the twelve tribes of Israel; with streets of transparent gold, reflecting like a mirror the thousands of beautiful mansions along their borders; with the river of life, and the throne of God and the Lamb at its source; with the tree of life yielding a different variety of luscious fruit each month in the year; and over it all the light of the slain Lamb, brighter than the noonday sun. Such is the home designed for Israel. None but the twelve tribes can enter the gates of the city; but all nations are represented in the vast multitude that throng its streets; for "it is now revealed unto his holy apostles and prophets by the Spirit; that the Gentiles should be fellow heirs, and of the same body, and partakers of his promise in Christ by the gospel."[1]

The unspeakable happiness of that period is represented by the words love, marriage, family, home. Taking first the family relation, we have the different members as follows: Christ is called the "Father" in Isa. 9:6. He is the head of the family. Paul states that the New Jerusalem above "is the *mother* of us all."[2] All the redeemed are the *children*, sons and daughters of the Almighty. "For this cause I bow my knees unto the Father of our Lord Jesus Christ, of whom the *whole family* in heaven and earth is named." Using the illustration of a wedding, we have the same parties expressed thus: Christ the bridegroom, the New Jerusalem the bride, and the church the guests. It is a very common error to suppose that the church is the "bride," an error which will be readily seen from the following text: —

And there came unto me one of the seven angels, . . . saying, Come hither, I will show thee the bride, the Lamb's wife. And he carried me away in the spirit to a great and high mountain, *and showed me that great city, the holy Jerusalem*, descending out of heaven from God.[3]

[1] Eph. 3:5, 6. [2] Gal. 4:26. [3] Rev. 21:9, 10.

By a strange inconsistency men have considered the city to be a figurative name for the church. The whole description is absurd when thus applied, but it is consistent when applied to a literal city. Furthermore, Christ distinctly said that in his Father's house were many mansions, and that he would go there and prepare a *place* for his people. There is a vast difference between the church and the city prepared for the church. Again, we read that when Abraham was called to leave home and country for "a place which he should after receive for an inheritance," he saw a "city which hath foundations, whose builder and maker is God." New Jerusalem, with "twelve foundations," built above and "adorned as a bride for her husband," exactly meets Abraham's expectations. Therefore the city is not a people, but it is the place for a people. Jerusalem above is the mother of the church. It is not the church; the people of God, who compose the church, are the children of the mother. But as surely as Jerusalem is the mother of us all, as Paul asserts, she must be the "bride," as John states. The redeemed are either children or guests, but they are not the mother nor the bride. The figure of marriage is several times taken to represent the close spiritual union between Christ and his church in this world; but this does not prove that they will actually and literally be the bride of the Lamb in the world to come, especially as the city is mentioned as the "bride, the Lamb's wife."

The contrast between the worldly Jerusalem, at one time the favored city, and the heavenly Jerusalem, still waiting for her hopes to be fulfilled, is set forth by Paul in an allegory concerning Hagar and Sarah. The former was only a bond-servant, while the latter was the lawful wife. By a human arrangement, an attempt was made to provide children for Abraham by Hagar, and Ishmael was born after the flesh; but Sarah was childless. These conditions made the bond-maid proud and haughty toward the wife. Finally her insolence became unbearable, and she and her son were sent away from the patriarch's family.

The application of this story of domestic life is obvious, as stated by the apostle. The true bride of Christ, the Lamb's wife, and mother of us all, is the *Jerusalem above*. But thus far she is childless and desolate. No happy children are in her home. Mansions are ready, but their occupants are absent. With more than a human mother's instinct, she cries, "Give me children, or else I die."

In the meantime an earthly city of Jerusalem, which God intended to be only a servant in the family, has come to claim the honored place of wife, and with arrogant pride demands that the family jewels shall be bestowed upon her and her illegitimate children. All the words of love addressed to the faithful, sorrowful wife are appropriated by the slave to feed her vanity. The long-suffering of God will at last be over, and the ungrateful woman and her seed will be expelled. In other words, when the earthly city and inheritance claim the distinction which belongs only to the heavenly home, the time of their eternal rejection is near and sure. An example of this has already been shown to the world in the destruction of the ancient city of Jerusalem, because in her pride she demanded the honor which is due to the Jerusalem above. Her people called themselves "Israel," simply because they were of national descent, as Ishmael was descended from Abraham; and they mocked at the children of faith, the true Israel, who set their hearts on a heavenly reward.

And so it is again in a larger degree. Even the Gentile nations now vie with one another in advocating the right of the rejected bond-servant, national Israel, again to usurp the place of wife and mother. They ignore the true Israel and the spiritual inheritance in the world to come. Promises made to the latter are coveted and stolen for the former. The return of the Jews and the promises to Israel absorb the attention of millions; but it is all a human arrangement. Eternal rejection of the worldly scheme is near, and waits only for the final call for true Israel to be given. The Eastern Question will culminate in that very thing. Then the children of faith, of all ages and nations, will be gathered to their heavenly home and to their waiting mother above.

Sing, O barren, thou that didst not bear; break forth into singing, and cry aloud, thou that didst not travail with child: for more are the children of the desolate than the children of the married wife, saith the Lord. Enlarge the place of thy tent, and let them stretch forth the curtains of thine habitations: spare not, lengthen thy cords, and strengthen thy stakes; for thou shalt break forth on the right hand and on the left; and thy seed shall inherit the Gentiles, and make the desolate cities to be inhabited. Fear not; for thou shalt not be ashamed: neither be thou confounded; for thou shalt not be put to shame: for thou shalt forget the shame of thy youth, and shalt not remember the reproach of thy widowhood any more. For thy Maker is thine husband; the Lord of Hosts is his name; and thy Redeemer the Holy One of Israel; The God of the whole earth shall he be called. For the Lord hath called thee as a woman forsaken and grieved in spirit, and a wife of youth, when thou wast refused, saith thy God. For a small moment have I forsaken thee; but with great mercies will I gather thee.[1]

There can be no doubt about these words applying to the Jerusalem above in contrast with the earthly Jerusalem; for Paul states this in Gal. 4:27, where he quotes part of the passage. The true city of God is represented as sorrowing because for a time she is apparently slighted by the Lord. With infinite tenderness he comforts her with words of love and the promise of many children. He praises her beauty and loveliness as follows: —

O thou afflicted, tossed with tempest, and not comforted, behold, I will lay thy stones with fair colors, and lay thy foundations with sapphires. And I will make thy windows

[1] Isa. 54:1-7.

of agates, and thy gates of carbuncles, and all thy borders of pleasant stones. And all thy children shall be taught of the Lord; and great shall be the peace of thy children.[1]

This language is similar to that in Revelation 21, where the foundations of precious stones and gates of pearl of the New Jerusalem are described. Still the lovely city mourns; for her children are yet pilgrims and strangers on earth, away from home, waiting for Jesus to come again and take them to her arms. Then the joy of the royal family will be complete.

Rejoice ye with Jerusalem, and be glad with her, all ye that love her: rejoice for joy with her, all ye that mourn for her. . . . As one whom his mother comforteth, so will I comfort you; and ye shall be comforted in Jerusalem.[2]

God has done great things for old Jerusalem and her children; but they have been cast off for cruel pride, and the time for the deliverance of the promised seed through the New Jerusalem draweth nigh. Reader, what do you say? Are your hopes still in old Jerusalem and the land of Palestine? or will you look to the New Jerusalem and the heavenly Canaan? According to your choice, so shall be the reward.

For Zion's sake will I not hold my peace, and for Jerusalem's sake I will not rest, until the righteousness thereof go forth as brightness, and the salvation thereof as a lamp that burneth. . . . Thou shalt no more be termed Forsaken;

---

[1] Isa. 54: 11–13.   [2] Isa. 66: 10, 13.

neither shall thy land any more be termed Desolate: but thou shalt be called Hephzi-bah, and thy land Beulah: for the Lord delighteth in thee, and thy land shall be married. For as a young man marrieth a virgin, so shall thy sons marry thee: and as the bridegroom rejoiceth over the bride, so shall thy God rejoice over thee. I have set watchmen upon thy walls, O Jerusalem, which shall never hold their peace day nor night; ye that make mention of the Lord, keep not silence, and give him no rest, till he establish, and till he make Jerusalem a praise in the earth.[1]

The relationship of all who are saved will be alike in that happy family. All are children; none are the bride. The city is the Lamb's wife; all the redeemed are her offspring. God does not show partiality among the saints by making a few the bride, and the rest only children. Each one is equally precious to him. The true church in the wilderness with Moses bears the same relationship to Christ as the true church in the present age. It is one body from first to last; one elect people in all ages; one true Israel out of all nations; with one Father, Jesus Christ, and of one holy mother, the New Jerusalem.

Indeed, we may go further and say that all the heavenly host, the holy angels, are likewise linked together with the human family in the wonderful plan of redemption: —

That in the dispensation of the fulness of times he might gather together in *one all things in Christ, both which are in heaven, and which are on earth; even in him.*[2] To the intent

---

[1] Isa. 62: 1–7.   [2] Eph. 1: 10.

that now unto the principalities and powers in *heavenly places* might be known *by the church* the manifold wisdom of God. . . . For this cause I bow my knees unto the Father of our Lord Jesus Christ, of whom the whole family in heaven and earth is named.[1]

Without indulging in unwarranted speculation as to the exact manner in which the inhabitants of heaven are concerned in our destiny, we may be sure from the above quotations that they are deeply interested in the church on earth. They are learning the manifold wisdom of God "according to the eternal purpose which he purposed in Christ Jesus our Lord." They are "all ministering spirits, sent forth to minister for them who shall be heirs of salvation;" they "desire to look into" the things which God has revealed to us by the prophets; and we are a "spectacle" unto them as well as to men. Now, we are a little lower than the angels, or a little while inferior to them; but Christ declares that those who are the children of the resurrection will be "equal unto the angels" in the world to come.

Now unto Him that is able to do exceeding abundantly above all that we ask or think, according to the power that worketh in us, unto him be glory in the church by Christ Jesus throughout all ages, world without end. Amen.[2]

[1] Eph. 3:10-15.   [2] Eph. 3:20, 21.

A FEW OF OUR BOOKS.

DANIEL AND THE REVELATION.

The Response of History To the Voice of Prophecy.

A verse-by-verse Study of these Important Books of the Bible.

BY URIAH SMITH.

DANIEL AND REVELATION are two of the most important books in all the Bible. This volume is a critical study of these books, verse by verse, designed to bring out the stirring, practical, and prophetic truths which they contain.

Many have considered these portions of Scripture hard to understand; but here a key is put into the reader's hand, which has made plain to thousands what was before dark and obscure. The field of history is carefully scanned, and its emphatic response to the voice of prophecy is shown to be clear and beyond dispute. A prophecy fulfilled (and there are many such in these books) is a most powerful antidote against skepticism.

Prophecy is still fulfilling. Scenes of the most startling nature are just before us, which all should understand.

757 Octavo Pages, Exclusive of 56 Full-Page Illustrations.

Cloth, marbled edges, - - $2.25   Library, marbled edges, $3.00
Cloth, gilt edges, - - - - 2.75   Full morocco, gilt edges, 4.50

IN FIVE LANGUAGES.   130th THOUSAND.

BY THE SAME AUTHOR.

Here and Hereafter, Or Man in Life and Death. (In two languages.) 5th edition, revised 1897; 11th thousand; 8vo, 357 pp.; cloth, $1.

Synopsis of Present Truth,—Or a Brief Exposition of the Views of Seventh-day Adventists. (In two languages.) 3d edition; 5th thousand; 8vo, 333 pp.; cloth, $1.

Modern Spiritualism: A subject of Prophecy and a Sign of the Times. 8vo, 156 pp.; illustrated, cloth, 50c.

Looking Unto Jesus. Or Christ in Type and Antitype. (Forthcoming.) Over 350 pp.; fully illustrated, cloth, $1.50.

Smith's Diagram of Parliamentary Rules. Pocket size, 32 pp., muslin, 50c.

Poem on the Sabbath: A Word for the Sabbath, or False Theories Exposed. 12mo, 64 pp., cloth, 30c.

COMPLETE COURSE IN FIVE BOOKS

THIS UNIQUE SERIES CONSISTS OF

BOOK ONE.— Primary Language Lessons from Life, Nature, and Revelation. Cloth, 50c.
BOOK TWO.— Elementary Grammar. 224 pages. Cloth, 65c.
BOOK THREE.— Complete Grammar. 281 pages. Cloth, 80c.
BOOK FOUR.— Rhetoric and Higher English. 375 pages. Cloth, $1.25
BOOK FIVE.— Studies in English Literature. (In preparation.)

THESE BOOKS CLAIM THE ATTENTION OF PRACTICAL EDUCATORS EVERYWHERE.

The ripe fruit of over forty years of varied experience in teaching language.

A NATURAL, PROGRESSIVE, COMPREHENSIVE AND THOROUGH METHOD IN ENGLISH.
FOR HOME STUDY.   FOR THE SCHOOLROOM.

By the aid of these books, energetic young men and young women can master the principles of the English language with little or no help from a teacher.

STEPS TO CHRIST.

A BOOK WHICH HAS CHEERED MANY A DISCOURAGED HEART.

BY MRS. E. G. WHITE.

PRESENTS in a simple and attractive manner the steps by which the sinner may be made complete in Christ. While the book is an excellent guide for inquirers and young converts, it also contains a wealth of counsel and encouragement for those who are laboring with the difficulties that beset a growing experience.

"A good book to put into the hands of an unconverted friend, as well as into the hands of a doubting church-member."—*The Western Recorder.*

"It is seldom the case that as unpretentious a volume as 'Steps to Christ' meets with such a cordial reception. . . . It contains just the words of counsel and encouragement which every young Christian needs. . . . The book is bound in an attractive manner, and the contents show that the author has a consecrated pen."—*The Midland Presbyterian.*

One Presbyterian pastor considered "Steps to Christ" so helpful that he purchased 300 copies to give to inquirers and others needing special help in his congregation.

Already Published in Fifteen Languages, as follows:—

English	German	French	Spanish	Italian
Holland	Danish	Swedish	Polish	Welsh
Portuguese	Hungarian	Rumanian	Bohemian	Finnish

New Enlarged Edition. 163 pp. Bound in fine cloth, with cover design embossed in aluminum. Price, post-paid, 60 cts.

A School Without Books

BY
Martha Watrous Stearns

IS a book that tells you how to have a school without a book! It gives you models from Mother Nature's own geometry — the crystals — and tells you how to study them, and how by studying them you can use your head, eyes, and hands in making a beautiful, naturally graded series of 32 useful, attractive articles, in pasteboard and straw, and it tells you how to weave common sense in all you do — even a basket.

Takes up the matter of child education from an entirely new standpoint, — the at-home method of training the child in lines which will bring practical results from the work done. This book teaches the children how to manipulate and transform crude materials into serviceable objects, thereby training their perceptions, ideals, and senses better than any other method possible to employ.

Every Teacher Wants **"A School Without Books"** To Make School Pleasant.
Every Mother Wants To Make Home Pleasant.
Every Child Wants To Make Him Pleasant.

194 8 x 9 Pages; Paper extra Fine; 26 Full-Page, Half-Tone Engravings; 16 Pattern Drawings. Also 20 Manilla Pattern Drawings, in separate package. Price, $1.50, Post-paid.

For complete Book Catalogues, English or Foreign, address —

REVIEW AND HERALD PUBLISHING COMPANY,
CHICAGO, ILL.; BATTLE CREEK, MICH.; ATLANTA, GA.

www.ingramcontent.com/pod-product-compliance
Lightning Source LLC
Chambersburg PA
CBHW031935230426
43672CB00010B/1931